THE SPIRIT OF ADOPTION

THE SPIRIT OF ADOPTION
At Home in God's Family

JEANNE STEVENSON-MOESSNER

Westminster John Knox Press
LOUISVILLE • LONDON

Book design by Sharon Adams
Cover design by Pam Poll Graphic Design
Cover illustration by Sister Olga, Communauté de Grandchamp, Switzerland, "Joseph, as Adoptive Father, with Jesus"

First edition
Published by Westminster John Knox Press
Louisville, Kentucky

This book is printed on acid-free paper that meets the American National Standards Institute Z39.48 standard. ♾

PRINTED IN THE UNITED STATES OF AMERICA

03 04 05 06 07 08 09 10 11 12 — 10 9 8 7 6 5 4 3 2 1

Library of Congress Cataloging-in-Publication Data

Moessner, Jeanne Stevenson, date
        The spirit of adoption : at home in God's family / Jeanne Stevenson-Moessner.— 1st ed.
        p. cm.
        Includes bibliographical references and index.
        ISBN 0-664-22200-5 (alk. paper)
        1. Adoption (Theology) 2. Adoptive parents—Religious life. 3. Adoption—Religious
aspects—Christianity. I. Title.

BT165 .M65 2003
261.8'35874—dc21

                                                                                    2002038075

To Jean McCarley Stevenson
The Great Adventurer

For This Child I Prayed

Hearts cried out in the darkness for you.
They have asked you of the Lord.[1]
The voiceless prayer offered from Hannah's moving lips has again been
                remembered by the Lord.

    "For this child I prayed; and the Lord has granted me the petition
              that I made to the Lord."[2]
You have been born to the blessed barren,
        and the womb that never bore,
and the breasts that never gave suck.[3]
    You are daughter to a mother,
        daughter to a father,
      sister to a brother.
Just as Jesus said from the cross,
      "Woman, here is your child. (Child), Here is your mother."[4]
You are adopted by those who did not bear you.
And from that hour they were in the same home. And so are you.

    "For this child I prayed; and the Lord has granted me the petition
              that I made to the Lord."
You are more than a child adopted into one family.
You are sister to those
        who have no sister,
          those who have sisters.
You are child to those
        who have no children,
          those who have children.
You are loved by those that you may only know as memories from someone's
    lips.
You are loved by those you have not yet met.

But a greater gift than all human love is yours.
You are a child of God.
We shout from voiceless moving lips,
    "See what love God has given us,
        that we should be called children of God;
    and so we are."[5]
And so you are, [name]
And so you are a child of God.
    For this child we prayed.
    For this, child, we prayed.

Jane E. Dasher, 1992

Contents

Foreword

The Spirit of Adoption is a book of theology, lightly disguised as a reflection on the adoption of children.

The Spirit of Adoption is an address to the issues surrounding adoption of children, heavily weighted toward theology.

Certainly, Jeanne Stevenson-Moessner's book will be of interest to families who have adopted, are adopting, or hope to adopt children. Around all such families are circles of relatives and friends who are drawn into the drama that adoption brings to those about whom they care, and they will be advised by these pages.

Less certainly, until one begins reading it and especially until one encounters the seventh chapter, her book should be of interest to individuals and communities formed by and focused on commitments of faith in God. To say that in that chapter "God as Adoptive Parent" comes across as a provocative metaphor is to say too little about her claims. In biblical revelation, as the author reads it and convincingly argues the case, the God who *is* love is also the God who *is* the Adoptive Parent. That is, the basic motion of God toward humans, in this reading, is adoptive.

Professor Stevenson-Moessner does not use exclamation points or bold-faced type, does not blow trumpets or take out billboards, to make her main theological point. She tells stories, and tells them well. They are not asides, fillers, or attention-getting illustrations of the sort preachers use when their sermon outlines sag. They *are* the point: The people who animate her narratives embody the travails and triumphs, the griefs and the joys—and these *always* come mixed—that we associate with adoption. She does not have to better the stories. They quietly make their point, her point.

Historians of religious subjects, this Foreword-writer among them, do not usually involve themselves with topics such as that of *The Spirit of Adoption*, unless they deal with the history, in this case, of adoption. While there are plenty of encounters with biblical history here, reaching past Esther to Hagar, for instance, and while there are some references to the development of adoption policies in the recent past, history is not the point here. So let me say how I came to be interested in this book, even to the point—let me admit this—of volunteering to write the Foreword.

The Association of Theological Schools, backed by the Henry Luce Foundation, initiated a program in which its juries each year select eight cream-of-the-crop proposals for advanced work by those who teach in eight disciplines in theological schools. I was privileged to chair the program in its first six years, and each round took the opportunity to learn what was coming, what was fresh, and who was adventuresome on this front. We referees would make our independent judgments and then meet. Almost always we concurred in our selection. There was no doubt that in her year in her field, Jeanne Stevenson-Moessner was the candidate.

This was one project on which I kept my eye, and when I met the author, I had her tell me the story, seasons before she made her oral progress report. Now I have the book, and it lives up to expectations. This is front-line work, on an urgent topic.

Second, my interest can be seen as an act of penitence. For decades I was the book review editor at *The Christian Century*, and had much say as to which books were reviewed. Some years ago an eloquent book on infertility reached the desk. I dismissed it out of hand, as "their," meaning someone else's, problem, not something with which the rest of us should bother during the years of the Civil Rights Movement and the Vietnam War. Some time later I chanced to meet the author, who, not asking for a review, kindly rephrased the book for me. I went back to read it and found it life-changing. Being in that majority company of couples who would be more concerned with limiting the number of births than with issues of fertility, I learned late of the depth of grief, anguish, and dashed hopes for the many and the heights of joy of the few.

The Spirit of Adoption deals with that issue.

Third, the Martys are in the zone of adoptive families. Forty years ago a social worker presented us with two children to foster. Their parents were alive. "You can't adopt, but given their birth-family situation, do know that they'll be part of your family for life." They are. Now we also thrill grandparently to the experience of adoption in another generation. Until I read this book, however, I had no theological pegs on which to hang the accounts of sufferings and glories that can come with adoption. Jeanne Stevenson-Moessner has gone a long way to supplying some.

The shocker that comes with this quiet book hit me in my conversation with

Jeanne. An inveterate dissertation-adviser, I asked her to finish the sentence all my advisees had to complete: "The thesis of my thesis is . . . "

She was clear and brisk and her answer was pointed. Had I ever thought of it that *biblically* we believers are all adopted, and that God is revealed more as Adopter than as Siring-Agent or Birth-Mother? Those are my terms, but they relate to her substance. Working from that realization, there are good reasons for all believers to take more seriously witness to that Adopter's role and to grow in empathy for families in the range of the adoption experience.

One more word: It would be a pity if the book had influence only on those intimately involved with adoption. Those who are at the margins can also profit. A friend who was a chaplain at a rehabilitation institute directly served people described as disabled or handicapped or other-abled, paraplegics and "wheelies" in their chairs. She convinced me that most of us who are related to such, who minister among them, who call on them or meet them in church, tend to make most of the wrong gestures, utter many of the worst phrasings, and fall short of finding the gifts that those in "rehab" had to offer. She has not yet written the book I look for, a kind of "how to" and "why to" relate.

The Spirit of Adoption is that practical kind of "how to" book on this subject on one level, and the "why to" theology work we have needed, on another. It is hard to think of any Christian who will have read it who will not have acquired new perspectives on adoption and on God as Adopter, perspectives that we sorely need and will surely welcome.

MARTIN E. MARTY
Fairfax M. Cone Distinguished Service Professor Emeritus
The University of Chicago

Acknowledgments

As I write these words of acknowledgment, a student of mine is en route to Beijing, China, to participate in an adoption. This student is accompanying her sister-in-law, who has been planning this journey toward her new baby daughter for many months. The two women will be met in Beijing by adoption social workers and translators and taken to a smaller city. There, in a hotel room, they will meet a baby girl who will become daughter to one, niece to the other. This is a homecoming worth the wait.

Writing this book has resemblances to this arduous and passionate adventure. Alexa Smith first conceived of the idea, while Stephanie Egnotovich of Westminster John Knox Press has orchestrated the details of the passage. She has done so with meticulous planning, concern, and foresight. The Henry Luce III Foundation granted me time off to bring this book home.

My family has set the context for my experience of adoption. My husband Dave is full of wisdom, and my children David and Jean are full of the joy of life. Linda Wlochal has tended to many practical and household responsibilities, freeing me for my research and writing. Robert and Anne Sayle have twice journeyed up and down the Mississippi River to be with us in the Midwest and connect us with home.

A book, like an international adoption, has an itinerary. There are places and people who facilitate the final phase of "homecoming." The Henry Luce Fellows at the 2001 conference in Princeton, the faculty at Austin Theological Seminary, and the Society for Pastoral Theology gave invigorating feedback along the way as the material was presented. In particular, I am indebted to Fred Craddock, Christopher Wilkins, Bonnie Miller-McLemore, Richard Hays, Scott Hendrix, Christine Blair, Kathryn Roberts, Carol Newsom, Luke Johnson, and John Alsup for specific insights that enhanced the final manuscript. Martin Marty gave the manuscript a final send-off and a blessing. The theological astuteness of Stephen Kolmetz has benefitted many and is evident in chapter 7. Jane Dasher's poetry and Connie Twining's sculpture have reiterated my themes in creative ways. Julie Tonini has brought these themes into production.

There were many facilitators at the University of Dubuque Theological Seminary, including work-study students Jennifer and Geoff Snook, Jim Bonewald, Mary Tryggeseth, Isaac Schrimpf, Lu LeConte, Nicky Story, and colleague Elizabeth Platt. There were a large number of interviewees to whom I promised anonymity. Please know that you are the heart of this work.

There is a retreat center in Gelterkinden, Switzerland, run by the Sisters of Grandchamp. It was there that I saw the original icon of Joseph, adoptive father, and Jesus, painted by Sister Olga. When I asked for copyright permission for use on the cover, the reply came, "If this would be a wonderful way to introduce your readers to the joy of the Scripture, we are also grateful for it, that we can share this joy!" I am honored by this generosity.

I dedicate this book to a woman whose gumption has far exceeded my expectations. When I arrived on a prop plane at a regional airport in Dubuque, Iowa, in a snowstorm in 1997, my first thought was, "My mother will never come visit us here." It does take maneuvering major airports and bad weather. Recently, en route from Memphis, she braved the ice storm of 2000, survived two days in Chicago's O'Hare airport, and was eventually bused into Dubuque just one hour before our daughter's ninth birthday party. When I was introducing my mother to the assembled third-graders and describing all the obstacles she had endured to get to that party, one mesmerized eight-year-old picked up his Dixie cup, and with reverence in his voice, toasted: "To the great adventurer!" She has never missed one of my children's birthdays or performances. I pick up this manuscript and echo the toast.

My student will arrive today in Beijing bearing gifts for those involved in the international adoption. I close this book with gifts, too. To adoptive parents, I give my understanding. To adoptees, I give encouragement. And to the birth parents, I give both an acknowledgment of their sacrifice and my deepest admiration.

JEANNE STEVENSON-MOESSNER

Introduction

Womb-love: God's mercy and compassion

For many, faith in the invulnerability of America shattered on September 11, 2001 along with the Twin Towers of the World Trade Center. Peace and security appeared as scattered as the rubble at Ground Zero. Out of the dimness came the candles of people of faith at services of worship, at vigils, at prayer services. We worshipped side by side with those from different denominations, independent churches, and faith traditions—united in our shock and grief and united as children of God. We worshipped as children in one household of faith.[1]

In our numbness, we turned to the familiar—the mercy and compassion of God. We nestled close to God, our Loving Parent, our only invincible and unshakable refuge. We needed the tender embrace of a God whose heart was also wounded. The mercy and compassion of God, this love in extremity, is literally translated as *womb-love*.[2] God's merciful compassion is God's *womb-love*. This womb-love is our most fundamental connectedness.

In a healthy parent-child relationship, there is a reflection of God's womb-love. When I use the word parent, I mean not only biological parents who nurture their physical offspring; I also mean birth parents who relinquish their children and adoptive parents who receive these children into their homes. You would expect the first two sets of parents to reveal glimpses of God's womb-love. This book is about adoptive parents and their womb-love for the children they have not borne.

We crave connectedness. We want to belong. We want to be "at home" somewhere, with someone. We desire to be known. That's why I have written this book.

I began writing this book in a mood of joy, immediately after experiencing the "homecoming" of a child. Homecoming is the day a child is placed in the home of an adoptive family or single parent. It can happen on very short notice, as little as 24 hours. Most likely, a prospective parent has anticipated the homecoming for a long time and has experienced some anxiety as well as elation. Whatever the variables, however, there is one constant: the wellspring of joy in the parent's heart. A homecoming of a longed-for child is parabolic for God's welcome of us, a glimpse of God's embrace, of God's hospitality. A placement or homecoming of a child often follows years of barrenness and infertility and is a celebration of gift in the adoption process.

After I wrote the early chapters of this book, I went through a failed adoption. I had not expected to have such pain in the adoption process. Even now, years later, we refer to 1991 as "the year we lost the baby." Because I now know that failed adoptions are not uncommon, I have incorporated this experience into the book and given it the name *miscarried adoption.*

My second draft continued the mood of joy, but incorporated as well the element of grief. As I increasingly realized the pain of a miscarried or failed adoption and observed the emotional and developmental difficulties adopted children face because of the fact of their relinquishment, I became aware that God's womb-love [mercy] combines compassion with suffering. I became aware that this God who cradles us is moved by all the moods of adoption. Ironically, it was the grief of adoption that thrust me most deeply into this throbbing womb, this creative center, of a tender God.

Complications and intricacies in raising an adopted child will also position an adoptive parent to both receive and channel God's unyielding compassion. As I now also know, adopted children have a higher rate of learning disorders, attention deficit hyperactivity disorder (ADHD), attachment disorder, and delinquent behavior than their non-adopted peers. Age at adoption, a history of early abuse or neglect, and the frequent shifting of foster care situations may contribute to attachment disorder and delinquent or antisocial behavior. In pre-adolescence, the implications of and anguish at having been relinquished by birth parents is usually a dawning awareness.

As our family began to live through some of these difficult aspects of adoption, I stopped writing this book. I felt my early chapters would mislead readers. Now, writing once again, I realize the first three chapters are a preamble to consider more deeply the passion of God, a God who contains the joy and the pain of loving a child, a God who offers a profound sense of continuity and connectedness through delight and dolor.

Many people desire children but cannot have them. When you come to accept the fact that you will not have a child, hope for offspring dies. A part of yourself extinguishes as well. Therefore, when a child is given to you, there is a resurrection of both hope and life itself. It is not so dissimilar from recovering from a near-fatal accident or illness, or beating the odds of a disease. When life is given to you again, your senses are sharpened and the commonplace becomes increasingly precious. The placement of a child in the home can be the occasion of such joy that the experience is sometimes labeled as mystical.

At the same time, increasing numbers of individuals and couples are adopting out of a sense of calling, of religious and humanitarian commitment. For them, more often than not, adoption means standing at the matrix of a human-divine encounter. Undertaken in partnership with the Creator of all life, adoption becomes a sublime undertaking.

The case studies and interviews in this book describe formalized adoptions. By that, I mean the placement of a child into a home with a legal process involving termination of birth parental rights, adoption papers, lawyers, and a court appearance. It is vital to note that some cultures and ethnic groups have practiced informal adoptions for years, especially working through the extended family or kin. Although this book describes formalized adoptions, it is important to recognize other ways children can be cared for and absorbed into a family unit.[3]

The increase in international, interracial, older, and special needs adoptions, coupled with heightened honesty among adoptive parents who are raising children, has led to greater openness regarding the various difficulties that can occur in the lives of adoptive families and developing adoptees. In the course of the interviews I conducted for this book, I heard stories containing both moments of ecstasy and times of despair. I have sought to articulate a theology that will stretch to both ends of this experiential spectrum, even as, most of the time, adoptive families actually function in the ordinary middle of the spectrum.

Reading this book will not make the process of adoption any less complicated. In fact, you may see adoption as a more complex phenomenon when the theological dimension is added. Media attention and articles on failed adoption enwrap the public. When an adoptive family has to return a child to the birth parents or parent, issues and emotions surface that affect all of us. The children caught in the middle force us to articulate our questions and focus our energies on the universal question: What really is parenting? What does it mean to be a parent? What is the ultimate significance of the nuclear family, that is, the biological family, the family of origin?

We also must ask, What does it mean to be adopted? Many of us know that we have to go outside the bonds and bounds of our nuclear families to receive the nurture we need. Nurturance comes in the form of mentors, models, surrogate mothers or fathers, spiritual directors, spiritual parents. What does it feel like to be nurtured as an adopted child? To tend and love a child as an adoptive parent? Whereas other books have concentrated on the facts and figures of adoption, in this book I expose the feelings people live through and with during the process of birthing a family through adoption.

For example, a psychology of adoption has already been written.[4] Psychiatric literature is now replete with articles on the subject of genetic and environmental influences on the adoptee. Sociological studies are assembling data to allow most of us involved with adoption to make informed choices and generally feel in the range of normal.[5] Psychologist and researcher Joyce Maguire Pavao has recently written on "normative crises in the development of the adoptive family" with an emphasis on the adopted child's development from birth to young adulthood.[6] What has been lacking in the literature, however, is an articulation of the role of faith as a resource that can motivate, undergird, and sustain those involved in adoption: birth parents, adoptees, and adoptive parents (the *adoption triad*).

Although I regularly refer to psychology, psychiatry, and sociology throughout this book, my task here is to write a theology of adoption. By this, I mean that I will reflect on and interpret God's involvement in the matter of adoption. As we move through a range of emotions and experiences, from joy to disillusionment, we will listen to the stories of adopting parents. Most of you will probably have a firsthand understanding of adoption, as a member of the adoption triad, or as a relative or good friend of someone in an adoption triad.

In chapter 1 I establish a central theme of the book: our identity as children of God and the church's role in establishing this understanding. Adoption will be presented as the overarching Biblical image for the invitation and inclusion of Gentiles in the Judaeo-Christian lineage. Thus, alongside the New Testament image of the new birth or second birth that Jesus described to Nicodemus as "being born again," I position the image of adoption. I am suggesting that the model and metaphor for the household of faith is best, although not exclusively, illustrated by the *adoptive family* or household.

Paralleling the process of physical birth, yet distinct from it, I develop chapters 2 through 6 in the following progression: the concepts of barrenness, conception, and expectant waiting, the "homecoming" or placement of a child, and the developing years of an adoptee. Chapter 7 begins to establish a theology of adoption: a religious articulation of issues such as divine kinship, the mutability and pathos of God, the pain of relinquishment, the naming of a child, and the household of faith. In a way, this chapter articulates a "transformative view" as described by Don Browning and Bonnie Miller-McLemore in *From Culture Wars to Common Ground.* "The transformative view says that for loyalty to the reign of God to be uppermost, family affections should be transformed, extended, and analogically applied to the wider community—indeed, extended all the way to the universal community or family of God."[7] Chapter 8 provides a Biblical basis for that theology. I believe that the diversity and complexity of some of the stories in the earlier chapters will convince you of the necessity of a theology to undergird those in the adoption triad.

The Many Faces of Adoption

In this book I develop adoption as a theological metaphor and propose an analogy or likeness between receiving a child into a home and entering God's family of faith. This metaphor undergirds the practical import of this book, which is to offer support, sustenance, spirituality, and "signposts" along the journey of adoption.

There are many configurations of "adopting families," and a sampling of adoptive parents open their lives to you through this book. This sampling will dispel the following myths: only couples can adopt; only heterosexuals can adopt; only persons having no biological children would want to adopt; adoptive parents are Caucasian. The adoptive parents whose voices are in this book will lead you into their accounts of successful as well as failed adoptions, private as well as agency adoptions, domestic and international adoptions. Even through a tangle of misgivings, miscarried adoptions, and misconceptions, their stories always include the sense of gift in receiving a child. At times, the sense of gift is overwhelming; it is always extensive.[8] Chapter 6 contains a number of these joyous accounts.

These couples and individuals who granted interviews will walk you gently through the book. Each story has a unique offering or contribution to the discussion of the various scenarios and settings of adoption. For the actual cases and people, I've changed names. Brief descriptions of interviewees may be helpful:

> Susan Hall, a single, working woman, following unsuccessful attempts at artificial insemination, adopted a daughter internationally, from Chile.
>
> Jane and Jim Rhodes, after seven years of treatments for unexplained infertility and two miscarried adoptions, experienced two successful domestic adoptions, one private and one through an agency.
>
> Theresa and Mike Russell, married graduate students, adopted privately following Theresa's emergency hysterectomy.

Darcy and Tom Algood, a biracial couple with three biological children, adopted a biracial child from the State Department of Human Resources.

Alicia Fox, a married woman with one biological child, developed a medical problem that precluded a second pregnancy; she adopted a child internationally.

Kathy Reiter, a single Caucasian lesbian in the Quaker tradition, experienced a miscarried international adoption in Peru. She later successfully adopted two African American infants with her partner.

Connie and Ed Gauley, foster parents, successfully adopted their foster child following a miscarriage.

Sam and Peggy Cesaretti have adopted two children internationally from Peru and Nepal.

Martha and Carl Brimmer, married with two biological children, experienced a miscarried international adoption (Korea).

Polly and Bob Austin are young parents with four special needs adopted children. Adoption was their first-choice option for building a family.

Dena Hogan, a single mother, twice went to Peru alone to adopt two children.

Jeff and Julie Sawyer, a married couple, adopted a son as an infant (five months) through domestic adoption.

Nan and Steve Brown adopted one infant through private domestic adoption and two infants through agency adoption.

Denise and Gerrit Van der Ven, a Dutch couple with four biological children, adopted a child from an orphanage while serving as educators in Indonesia.

Linda and Harry Turnbull, lawyers, adopted internationally and had a biological child.

These adoptive parents speak out of their successful vulnerabilty. That vulnerability involves an openness to the painful realities of infertility, miscarriage, and failed adoptions, and to the mysterious workings of the God who stands at the periphery of pain. Theirs are stories of faith. They are stories of failure. They are stories of faith through failure. In all but one case, the individuals persisted until the adoption process culminated in the homecoming of a child.

This book is written by an adoptive mother with adoptive parent(s) in mind. I hope that adolescent and adult adoptees, as well as birth parents, will draw encouragement from this book. The love, dedication, and persistence of the interviewees emanate not only from the pages of their stories, but from the chapters of their lives. Their faith, like the binding and cover of a book, holds the chapters together.

One seminary couple was held together by a song of faith taken from Isaiah. The refrain in "Here I Am, Lord," a hymn written by Daniel L.Schutte in 1981, is an adaptation of Isa 6:8–9:

> Then, I heard the voice of the Lord saying, "Whom shall I send, and who will go for us?" And I said, "Here am I; send me!"

In the hymn, God does various things, one of which is to break hearts of stone and turn them into love alone. The question is always, "Whom shall I send?" Repeatedly, the seminary couple responded to the call that for them first resulted in the adoption of three siblings (twelve-year-old boy and girl twins and their ten-year-old brother), then six years later another set of twin boys (age six), then four years later another sibling group (five-year-old girl and four-year-old boy). When I interviewed the adoptive mother, she disclosed all of the issues that these seven children had dealt them post-adoption: learning disabilities, retardation, sexual abuse, speech impediments, attachment disorder, violent behavior, one prison sentence for sexual misdemeanor, running away, rape, group homes. When I asked the adoptive mother how she had endured all of this, she confided: "I looked back many, many times. I said, 'God, how do you possibly think I can do this?' I never lost sight of [my belief] that God put these children in my hands, especially these harder ones. Many times I would say, 'I just don't know that I can do this.' What kept me going was this song." She saw and continues to see adoption as her calling.

One of her boys was asked by their youth director to give a sermon. This particular son had been sexually abused by his biological father and had acted out in aggressive and inappropriate ways with his adoptive family. He had been a difficult child. Yet, after he preached, he ended with the hymn, "Here I Am, Lord," and said: "This song has been very special to my mom and dad. They took all of our hearts of stone and turned them into love alone."

The Adoptive Family

As recently as fifteen years ago, adoption agencies and social workers involved in the adoption process maintained a stance called "rejection-of-difference."[9] That belief held that there was no difference between a family with biological children and a family with adopted children. Medical records were sealed, birth certificates were falsified, all in an attempt to ensure that adoptive parents' experience replicated that of birth parents.

Social workers know now that this is not the case. Parenting adopted children is often like piecing together a puzzle with major portions missing. The major pieces can include significant parts of a child's medical history or heritage. With the increase in international, interracial, older, and special needs adoptions, coupled with heightened honesty among adoptive parents who are raising children, there is now greater openness regarding difficulties that can occur in the lives of the adoptive families and developing adoptees. Social workers and agencies are now educating prospective adoptive parents that bringing a child into the home through adoption is not the same as having a biological child. This in no way means that the loving is not as profound. It means there may be issues of primal wounding, grieving and loss, and complication to the identity search in the adolescent years. It means adoptive parents will probably not have children who look like them physically, act like them behaviorally, or perpetuate certain abilities and innate talents. The healthy adoptive family moves through experience into an informed position called "acknowledgment-of-difference."[10] In this way, the adopted child, surrounded by loving nurture, is free to become herself, himself.

No other model better suits the church than that of the healthy adopted family. Often through pain and disenchantment, the loving adoptive family releases certain expectations and embraces what they have been given. This is a profound love of which I speak, and it can be born of much loss and patience. There is also a great joy in loving freely. It is my hope that as we who are Christians live into the spiritual reality of our adoption, we can emulate the acknowledgment and acceptance-of-differences that a healthy adoptive family models.

The Ends in Sight

The Spirit of Adoption: At Home in God's Family was written to support families in adoption and to formulate a theology of adoption that is applicable to Christian churches. I have seven goals in writing. The first is to embolden Christians to rely on a Biblical, anthropological mirror in which to see themselves as adopted sons and daughters "beloved of God." The second is to encourage the church as a family or household of faith to develop its ecclesiology to include a healthy acknowledgment and acceptance-of-differences among all its members as demonstrated by the resilient and flexible families in our society who have adopted children and embraced dissimilarities. Thus, I offer to an increasingly fragmenting church a model that will help in its divisive dysfunction.

The third goal is to place, in confessional terms, the concept of Biblical adoption alongside those of justification and sanctification.[11] No longer should commentaries on Romans, Galatians, and Ephesians be written without more attention to this unifying image. Fourth, I seek to redirect attention to the writings of earlier theologians such as Augustine and Irenaeus on the subject of adoption. Fifth, I will extend our images of God to include Adoptive Parent as well as Birthing Parent (see Eph. 1:5, Rom. 8:15, and Gal. 4:4–5).

Sixth, I seek to offer supportive insight to families involved in actual adoption of children. Seventh, I hope that more of us involved in adoption dynamics—as clergy, as an adoptive parent, as a grandparent, as a neighbor or friend—will be drawn into God's womb-love. When, as Christians, we take the name of "adopted children of God," we also intentionally identify with those who have been marginalized by our society. We become emboldened to say to those who have no home and no birthright in society, "I will add your name to my name so that we can be seen to belong together, with Christ the Firstborn, at home in God's family."

Before this book went to press, I was asked to lead a workshop at a conference where the overall theme was "navigating differences." A plenary speaker presented a macrocosmic view of exclusion and privilege, largely along racial and ethnic lines. I presented the healthy adoptive family as a *microcosmic* example of acceptance and navigation of differences. It is the "lack of biological relatedness" in adoptive families that creates such a pervasive need for this embrace of differences.[12] During my workshop, Martin Simms, a teacher from New Hampshire, told the following story of the funeral of his wife's grandmother, a story illustrating an unhealthy family situation with rejection-of-differences along bloodlines.

"My wife's grandmother is in a line of people who have taken genealogy very seriously. She is part of a strain that goes back to English roots. My wife's mother is a member of The Colonial Dames. They have to document their heritage back to the 1500s. The genealogy factor has always been there. At the funeral there was a call to get together for a photo of the descendants of [the deceased]. My wife was sitting with our [adopted] daughter, Marilyn, on her lap. The photographer, a family member, said: 'No, Marilyn will not be a part of this picture.' As my wife and I thought about it later, we realized Marilyn was not a blood descendant of the deceased. We let our hurt be known. There was no successful resolution."

Many dedicated people like Martin have come forward with their stories, from which I have selected representative experiences. I am appreciative of everyone who gave of their time both in interviews and in feedback to my early presentations on the topic of adoption.

As you read, I hope you will sense the presence of a God whose heart beats to each throb of your own. I trust that you, too, will be drawn into the embrace of your own adoption.

Chapter 1

The Trembling Womb

Therefore, my womb trembles for him [Ephraim]:
I will truly show motherly-compassion upon him.[1]

Jeremiah 31:20

"*M*y wife and I were on vacation in Gatlinburg and over to our table came this old man who was a greeter and, I learned later, a part owner of The Black Bear Inn. He said 'Good evening,' and we said, 'Good evening,' and he asked where we were from; we were at that time in Oklahoma. And then he asked what I did. I was getting a little irritated because he was a stranger, and he didn't need all that. But when I told him I was a minister, he said, 'I have a story about a minister' and pulled out a chair and sat down at our table. Uninvited by the way, but it's his business. I thought he was going to tell a joke; everybody has a joke about a minister. I thought, he's going to tell one, and I would pretend I had never heard it and smile, and he would go away.

"At any rate, he said, 'I was born not far from here, out from the village of Cosby, in a place called Laurel Springs. My mother was not married. The children at school made fun of me. I ate my lunch alone. I hid during recess because they said ugly things to me. When I went to town, people looked at my mother and me. I just figured they were trying to make guesses as to who was my father. So I had a very painful childhood. In the course of it, I started going—about middle school age—to Laurel Springs Christian Church back in the woods; it had kerosene lamps. There was an old preacher there with a long beard, a chiseled face, and a deep voice. I liked to hear him preach but I didn't want to be embarrassed. I would just go for the sermon and rush out. I did that for some time. One day some of the people gathered in the aisle, and I couldn't get by, and I felt this hand on my shoulder, and I looked around and I could see the face and the beard of the preacher. I was scared to death because I was always afraid of being embarrassed in public. He stared at me as though he was trying to guess what man in the community was my father. After he looked at me carefully, he said, "Boy you are a child of . . ." He paused there. I just froze. "Boy, you are a child of . . . God. I see a striking resemblance." He swatted me on the bottom and said, "Go claim your inheritance." That was really the first day of my life.'

"I said, 'your name again?' He said, '[a governor, twice-elected].' I remembered my father talking about the people of Tennessee twice electing [this man] as governor of the state although he was called publicly, especially by the political opposition, the 'bastard governor.' My father said, 'The people of Tennessee twice elected a bastard governor . . .'

"The former governor wanted his story told. He said to me, 'My papers are at the University of Tennessee and will be published after my death, and I have asked that my story be told as the preface as encouragement to other children born here in the mountains, children of "questionable background."'

"That was [the former governor]. It was that expression, 'you are a child of God, I see a striking resemblance. Go claim your inheritance,' that stays with me. That was one of the most moving experiences I ever had. It came as such a surprise especially when I was resisting his even being there, interrupting our evening meal. That was quite a moment. It is a true and remarkable story."[2]

As this story told to me by Fred Craddock recalls, one fundamental definition of a Christian is a "child of God." That identity is the substructure of Christian spirituality, the fundament of Christian faith, the foundation of Christian self-concept. It is the overarching and undergirding characterization of who we really are. I believe that the adoption process in microcosm reflects the macrocosm of becoming family or household of God as we become part of the genealogy of Jesus Christ. As adoptive parents learn as they raise their children, adopted children often must deal with severe abandonment issues and with complicated identity and intimacy crises. Statistics show that adopted children are overrepresented in therapy.[3] According to the director of Chestnut Lodge Hospital, a residential adolescent treatment program in Rockville, Maryland, adopted children are "at risk with more than a ten-to-one chance for psychosocial maldevelopment as compared with offspring raised entirely by their own parents within their own families."[4] In this book I offer a theological foundation from which to draw in such crises and in therapy.

In the true story, above, the title "child of God" overcame the demeaning label, "bastard child." The nomenclature "child of God" is the essential, definite, pervasive, and ultimate demarcation of The-One-to-Whom Christians belong. It supercedes biological ties and relationships. The label "child of

God" can be transformative, as it was in the case of the twice-elected governor of Tennessee who began to image himself in a different way and to "claim his inheritance" once it had been given to him. As in his case, the re-imaging of one's self as child of God can not only impact present functioning, but also reconfigure the way the past is viewed and fortify a person for the future.

Jesus himself encouraged his followers' identity as children of God. Each of the Gospels contains a clue as to why this is so. When, as a twelve-year-old, Jesus spoke of his Father's house in reference to the temple in Jerusalem, he was implying that he had a higher allegiance to God than to his earthly parents, who had come to Jerusalem for the feast of the Passover. As an adult, as recorded in Matthew and in Mark, when his mother and brothers came looking for him, Jesus asserted: "For whoever does the will of my Father in heaven is my brother and sister and mother" (Matt. 12:50; Mark 3:35). In the Gospel of John, Jesus joined Mary and the disciple John at the foot of the Cross in a newly reconfigured family (19:27). What we see introduced in the Gospels, then, is a new household of faith into which one can enter only as a child (Matt. 19:14). Although the church has long understood that a person enters the family of faith as a spiritual child, it has failed to recognize that the New Testament primarily portrays entry into the family of faith *as adopted children*!

The Church: Time to Lead

Our daughter brought home her fourth-grade reading assignment, a Scholastic publication titled *Karen's School Picture.*[5] She was disturbed over the chapter, "Mean Things to Do to Ricky Torres." In this chapter, an angry Karen writes a list of retaliatory gestures toward Ricky Torres, the "pest" in her second-grade classroom. Karen's list of horrible things included the following:

"1. Tell him he smells.
2. Put my strawberry eraser in his desk and tell Ms. Coleman he stole it.
3. Put a worm in his lunch box.
4. Put pepper (lots of it) in his lunch box.
5. Tell him his eyes have turned orange.
6. Hide his reading book.
7. Tell him that Mollie Foley from Mrs. Fulton's room says she's in love with him and wants to kiss him on the playground.
8. Tell him he's adopted."

As this list illustrates society's prevalent image of adoption is still that of a second-class option. Education may attempt to alter concepts, but it is more difficult to alter an image. In *Karen's School Picture*, Karen's image of adoption is that it is an embarrassment, a horrible occurrence. According to church educator Nelle Morton, images are absorbed from infancy through one's development. A concept is learned. For an image to be altered, it must be, as Morton puts it, "shattered." Only then can an image be replaced.[6]

Perhaps the church has been influenced by our historic cultural tendency to image adoption as a second-class substitute for biological birth. Perhaps the church has succumbed to and participated in the culture's idolatry of the fertile family with biological children. The consequences of this attitude, however unintentional, are exclusion and pain.

Until recently, the subconscious image most people in contemporary western culture called up when they thought of family has been a biologically constructed one. Most of us are not aware that such images shape many of our concepts from infancy. And the church is not exempt from such thinking. Ministers often speak out of such unquestioned images. Father Ron is an example. He was preaching on Col. 1:15: "He [Christ] is the image of the invisible God, the firstborn of all creation." Because it was Wednesday mass at the Catholic school, the congregation was primarily made up of children, kindergartners through eighth-graders, with a sprinkling of teachers, administrators, and parents like myself.

Father Ron meant well. He was kind-hearted and would never have intentionally excluded any of the children from his sermon. His homily went like this: Children look like their parents; Jesus as God's Son reveals what God is like. Father Ron gave examples: "Maybe you look just like your mother. You have her eyes, her nose, her dimple." "Perhaps you are an athlete just like your uncle Sam. You have his genes." The point was profoundly simple: We know what God is like by looking at Jesus.

But the actual and complex reality was not lost on the two third-grade girls seated directly in front of me. Both were dark-skinned, one from India and one from Southeast Asia, and both had Caucasian parents. The more passionately Father Ron spoke, the more pointedly one of the girls shook her head "No" in rhythm with his preaching. The Catholic school had a substantial number of adopted children, yet Father Ron preached on and on to only the biological familes.

Two-thirds of the way through the sermon, he realized his miscalculation and changed tack. He acknowledged that there were children in the church who had been adopted into families and asked them to raise their hands high. But not every child wanted such attention, and now, reluctant children were confronted with a choice: hide their identity from the priest, or reveal an aspect of themselves that some children consider personal or private. Hands went up at half-mast in the sea of his insensitivity and their uncertainty.

Father Ron was known as a gentle priest. He did not mean to exclude some of the children in his sermon. He was simply unaware that he was operating out of an image of biological family. Father Ron was not aware that he had constructed his sermon illustrations from this image of family as physically related. Just as Father Ron had not intended to be hurtful, the church is also not ill-intentioned. It has at various times acknowledged that some families are constituted through adoption. As international adoptions increase, as attention is given to high-profile celebrity adoptions, as communities see families adopted interracially, the culture is becoming increasingly receptive to these new blended families. The church is following the lead of the American culture. But despite the best of intentions, without sensitivity, an ecclesiastical disaster can occur.

Sociologist Christine Swientek documents such a disaster. She provides another example of a well-intentioned pastor's ineptitude and inappropriateness in dealing with an adopted child. She tells how, one Thursday afternoon, fourteen-year-old Hannes went with his friends to confirmation class, as they had been doing for months. The pastor spoke that day about being "children of God" and looked about for an example to illustrate this special relationship between father and children. He looked at Hannes, and in front of thirty-five chattering, snickering, and giggling adolescents said: "You should try to imagine what it is like to be Hannes at home—his parents are not his birth parents. Hannes' parents are his adoptive parents who took him and raised him. They do not love him any less."[7]

Hannes, who did not have the slightest idea that he was adopted, was dumbfounded. He stood up, walked outside, and ran away. No one saw him for three months. At home, his loving and frightened adoptive parents sat bewildered, for they had done as they had been coached by the adoption counselors. They had kept the adoption a secret. No one had ever helped them know how, when, or even that they should inform Hannes about his adoption. It is not clear in Swientek's case study exactly how the pastor found out this apparently confidential information.

When Hannes was eventually found, he was in juvenile detention for stealing food from a supermarket. He had been sleeping on park benches, in deserted buildings, and in garden sheds. He had survived by stealing from supermarkets and small gardens. He was unkempt and dirty. He had stayed within forty miles of his house. Although Hannes' case was handled by a criminal investigator who took a fatherly interest in him, the psychological damage done to Hannes was extensive. A pervasive sense of distrust of the world around him caused Hannes to retreat within himself and distance himself from others. He entered the underworld of crime.

These stories and others like them illustrate both the secrecy and the insensitivity that has surrounded adoption. In both actual instances, the ministers did not view adoption as normative. In the case of Father Ron, adoption was excluded as a normative way to constitute a family. In the second illustration, Hannes' pastor singled out Hannes as different from the norm of biological children. The pastor may also have broken a confidence, for Hannes' parents were keeping a secret. Until very recently, such secrecy has generally been condoned and even supported by society and the social work system. The Christian churches, by and large, have followed secular cultural trends. As the twenty-first century begins, these churches have the opportunity to lead the discussions and provide spiritual sensitivity in the adoption process. After all, for most families who belong to a church or synagogue, their faith is at the very center of an adoption. It is time for the church to lead.

Adoption as Metaphor

The church has long emphasized the theological concept of "being born again," the reality of the "new birth" or second birth. This concept, which makes its way regularly into sermons and evangelical outreach, is based on a conversation in John 3:3–5 between a Pharisee named Nicodemus and Jesus:

> Jesus answered him [Nicodemus], "Very truly, I tell you, no one can see the kingdom of God without being born from above." Nicodemus said to him, "How can anyone be born after having grown old? Can one enter a second time into the mother's womb and be born?" Jesus answered, "Very truly, I tell you, no one can enter the kingdom of God without being born of water and Spirit. What is born of the flesh is flesh, and what is born of the Spirit is spirit."

Particularly in the Southern religious circuit, this metaphor of the second birth is propounded from pulpits, in Sunday School curriculae, and in seminaries.

And, unfortunately, the church has at the same time underemphasized another central theme in the canon of Scripture—adoption. Adoption is the overarching Biblical image for the invitation and inclusion of Gentiles in the Judeo-Christian lineage as family of God. The book of Ephesians describes us as chosen in love to be adopted by God as children through Jesus Christ, according to the kind intention of God's will:

> [God] destined us for adoption as his children through Jesus Christ, according to the good pleasure of [God's] will. (Eph. 1:5)

With that adoption, as Eph. 1:7–14 shows, riches are lavished upon us, an inheritance is obtained, and the Holy Spirit is given as a pledge to that inheritance.

Leaders in the early church alluded to adoption. In his thoughts on becoming "sons of God," for example, the theologian and church father Augustine clearly denied being born of God's substance through generation, arguing instead for a doctrine of deification through adoption. The image of God, he maintained, can be lost from within a person or can be deformed. Our participation in Christ's nature through baptism can heal that deformity, and the image of God can be restored in us.[8] A person can become a child of God, and thus, a god (see Ps. 82:6). Augustine used the word *deification* to mean "becoming an adopted child of God":

> It is clear that [God] calls [people] *gods* through their being deified by [God's] grace and not born of [God's] substance. . . . For to them gave [God] power to become [children] of God. If we are made [children] of God, we are also made gods; but this is done by grace of adoption, and not by generation.[9]

Augustine's doctrine of deification by adoption was overshadowed by his own work and that of later theologians on the doctrines of justification and sanctification. The idea of adoption did not, however, completely disappear in the church's writings. For example, in the Westminster Confession of Faith (1647), lodged between the chapters "Of Justification" and "Of Sanctification" we find the small but crucial chapter "Of Adoption":

> All those that are justified, God vouchsafeth, in and for his only Son Jesus Christ, to make partakers of the grace of adoption: by which they are taken into the number, and enjoy the liberties and privileges of the children of God; have his name put upon them; receive the Spirit of adoption; have access to the throne of grace with boldness; are enabled to cry, Abba, Father; are pitied, protected, provided for, and chastened by him as by a father; yet never cast off, but sealed to the day of redemption, and inherit the promises, as heirs of everlasting salvation.[10]

More recently, even the late Sigmund Freud, who criticized religion on many fronts, nonetheless acknowledged that religion had three positive functions, one of which was the reduction of the overimportance and idolatry of the biological family: "[religion] lowered the importance of [the child's] family relationships, and thus protected [the child] from the threat of isolation by giving [the child] access to the great community of [humankind]. The untamed and fear-ridden child became social, well-behaved, and amenable to education. The chief motive force of the influence which religion had upon [the child] was [the child's] identification with the figure of Christ."[11]

Despite such clear support, the Christian tradition has long had an unconscious aversion and defensive reaction to the notion of adoption. As a consequence, it has avoided the topic. Like the avoidance mechanisms practiced by the church, some parents, like Hannes', hide from their children the fact of their adoption. They dread the moment of telling for a variety of reasons. Most often, they are fearful that in some way the child will be hurt. Parents know how cruel children can be and may hope that by withholding information they can protect their children from taunts. Adoptive parents remember casual but callous comments made about birth parents, comments like the one we have all heard in reference to an unwed mother: "She is really a good girl. She just made a mistake." The inference is that the child born of this single woman and placed for adoption is, therefore, a mistake. Caring adoptive parents would never want their son or daughter to grow up with the idea they were a mistake, but they recall how often voices lower at the admission, "She's adopted." The word "adopted" is used as a qualifier, an adjective, whereas "biological" is not. Most non-adoptive parents do *not* introduce their child in this way: "She's biological."

How can the church lead the way in demonstrating our belonging as children of God? How can the church offer a critique of society's elevation of the genetically related, nuclear family while affirming the need for connectedness—familial connectedness? How can the church explore contemporary correctives to the culture's idolatry of the biologically defined family without being misunderstood as undermining those families? How can religion open us to the community of humankind? How can we be God's household of faith?

The book of Ephesians, which we look at in chapter 8, contains insight into these provocative questions. Ephesians startles us into the awareness that, from a Biblical standpoint, we too are adopted. This recognition gives us a perspective outside of our nuclear families or our families of origin. This realization of our adoption becomes the groundwork for theological discussion of what it means to be family or household of God, of what it means to participate in the community of humankind. Ephesians offers us a basis for our experiences as those impacted by the actual praxis of adoption.

Gift, Guilt, Grief: An Adoption Triad

There are many feelings in adoption. The adoption process involves the powerful interplay between a sense of grief and a sense of gift; the feeling of sadness in grief and the feeling of joy in receiving a gift make themselves felt throughout the lives of all involved in adoption. Grief manifests itself in various ways. Birth parents grieve the loss of their child; the loss becomes "an irrepressible sorrow."[12] Some birth mothers refer to an earlier decade in which adoption was a forced option. Children later grieve the loss of their biological parents and that unreplaceable piece of their lives, forming a "primal wound."[13] Adoptive parents grieve their inability to relate to the conception, pregnancy, and possibly the birth of their child. Adoptive parents may have missed the early months and years of their children's lives entirely. Adoptive mothers may mourn their inability to have carried this child in utero. There are many nuances of grief.

Whereas many social workers emphasize the elements of grief common to birth parents, adoptees, and adoptive parents, I focus also on the reality of gift, which is as consistently a life-long companion as the grief. From a theological perspective, the sense of gift permeates the grief process of adoption. The grief comes in giving up the child, giving up the expectation of having a child, or from being given up as a child. Birth parents generally feel they have given the gift of life to their child. Birth parents who relinquish their children for adoption believe that in making an adoption plan, they are setting up the best care for their child. This movement of relinquishment is not so far removed from the belief, "For God so loved . . . that [God] gave [God's] only Son" (John 3:16). Adoptive parents acclaim that the placing of a child in their home is the greatest human gift they have ever received.[14] The children, in later years, have varying reactions to the knowledge that they were "given up" as a gift in adoption. On one hand, they may feel a dawning awareness of the love behind the giving and receiving; on the other hand, they may focus solely on the relinquishment and feel anger. These feelings tend to surface when the children cognitively understand the concept of adoption (preteen years), during their struggle for identity formation (in the teenage years), or on the occasion of the birth of the adoptee's first child (young adulthood).

Amidst the feelings of both sadness and joy that grief and giftedness bring with them, there is also an element of guilt in the adoption process. For example, the adoptee involved commonly feels guilty toward the adoptive parents for desiring search and reunion with the birth parents. Birth parents often demonstrate subsequent ambivalence about their actions and may feel guilt that they were unable to provide the care required for the child. Adoptive parents can be made to feel guilty that they were part of the network that took a child away from the biological mother. This book will continue to follow the themes of grief, guilt, and gift as they surface in various ways.

However, even as I acknowledge these themes in adoption—gift, grief, and guilt—, I must underscore the overarching perception of "gift" that was at the center of all the interviews I have conducted. From the parents' point of view, the motivation for what they have done has come from the tender love of and for a child. The only way to describe their emotion is by the Biblical term *womb-love*. Womb-love [*rechem*] is synonymous in the Old Testament with the mercy and compassion of God [*rahum*]. Suggesting God as a Mother with love and nurture for children, the maternal image of mercy or womb-love is used.

> Therefore, my womb [*rechem*] trembles for him [Ephraim]:
> I will truly show motherly compassion [*rahum*] upon him.
>   (Jer. 31:20, trans. Phyllis Trible)

Womb-love or motherly attachment is God's compassion, continual and constant, even to straying children.[15] This book is about love, womb-love that is not devoid of pain. Womb-love is how God loves, and the adoptive parents in this book will give glimpses of what that is like.

The movie "Immediate Family," a story of an open adoption, shows the womb-love of both the birth parents and the adoptive parents for a newborn. This connectedness to the womb was demonstrated when the birth mother allowed the prospective adoptive couple to place their hands on her abdomen as the fetus moved and kicked. It was equally evident when birth and adoptive mothers danced together to a familiar tune. It was most evident when the birth mother insisted in the delivery room that the adoptive father cut the umbilical cord. Womb-love, that yearning from the very center of one's being, describes a tenacious compassion that is used to illustrate God's desire and mercy.

> Look down from heaven and see,
>   from your holy and glorious habitation.
> Where are your zeal and your might?
>   [The trembling of your womb][16] and your compassion?
> They are withheld from me."
>   (Isa. 63:15, amended NRSV)

A homecoming of a longed-for child is parabolic for God's welcome of us. It is a glimpse of God's embrace, of God's hospitality, of God's trembling womb. It reminds us and draws us to a Biblical concept we have neglected: As we enter the family of faith, we too are adopted. To be a child of God is to be adopted.

Chapter 2

"Give Me Children, or I Shall Die!"
(Gen. 30:1)

When Rachel saw that she bore Jacob no children, she envied her sister; and she said to Jacob, "Give me children, or I shall die!" Jacob became very angry with Rachel.

(Gen. 30:1)

Sam Cesaretti: "We'd been married for thirteen years before we adopted. For several years we tried to have children, and we couldn't. That whole process was just one of the most agonizing processes, not just for Peggy but for me, the father, for me, as well. The stuff you have to go through. We didn't go all the way to in vitro fertilization. We had made a conscious decision not to do that for a number of reasons. The process is in some ways almost dehumanizing. You know—'I want you to go home and at 7:30, I want you to make love, and then I want you to come back to the clinic.' Time and again, of course, the tests came up negative."

Nan Brown: "We found out about five years into our marriage that we couldn't have children. Our adoption experience started then . . . Steve, my husband was very willing to go along with that because we wanted a huge family . . . All of our friends were having children, and that was the most difficult thing to deal with. I was in a small Bible study with six young women who all wanted babies. I was the only one who could not have babies. God gave me such peace about it . . . God gave me real joy for my friends and excitement for their pregnancies and births. I had some tears. . . . I can look back on that time with some pain, but some real joy because I knew God was faithful.

"The verse that I claimed throughout this whole thing was Jer. 29:11–13! 'For surely I know the plans I have for you, says the LORD, plans for your welfare and not for harm, to give you a future with hope. Then when you call upon me and come and pray to me, I will hear you.' I knew that God was not going to leave me without children, whether that meant having our own or working with children in some way. When we found out that we could not have [biological] children, it was a very-cut-and-dried situation. Steve would be very up front with you and tell you it's him. But when medical tests told us unequivocally that we could not have children, we knew we could go on with our lives . . . I know Steve felt guilty, and yet he was able to work through all that. And I tell him to this day that we would never have the kids we have if it wasn't for him. We love our kids, and we wouldn't want any others."

Linda Turnbull: "We were trying to adopt at the same time we were still going through efforts to have a biological child. This happened over a period of so many years—fifteen. We thought we were at the end of the road. We abandoned the idea. We were very sad. We were trying to reconcile ourselves to a life without children."

Harry Turnbull: "We settled into an empty-nester lifestyle; but we were never comfortable with that."

Kathy Reiter, a teacher, decided at age thirty-four to adopt as a single parent. Her attitude demonstrates an essential and important insight: Adoption is the first choice, Plan A, for many. For Kathy, Plan B would have been artificial insemination. Kathy's first attempt at international adoption failed. In that effort, she first saw "her baby" in an orphanage in Peru, limp and lifeless. He had been found on the grounds of a public hospital, suffering from severe malnutrition. She cared for him in Peru for three months. "In some ways I was really afraid to love him. I was very attached to this baby. He was definitely my child."

A Peruvian judge ruled against the adoption, and Kathy lost both her subsequent appeal and the baby, an event she likens to a kidnapping. She eventually adopted two American black children, who were three years and ten months at the time of our interview. Between one-fourth and one-half of the children in her Quaker congregation in a major city are adopted. "Adoption is often seen as a second choice. For us, it was a first choice. We have strong feelings that the important part of parenting is raising the child."

The Curse of Barrenness

Give them [their due], O LORD—
    what will you give?

Give them a miscarrying womb
    and dry breasts.
                    (Hos. 9:14)

In Scripture, dry breasts and a miscarrying or infertile womb are signs of God's disfavor. Scripture abounds with stories of the curse of barrenness and the numerous efforts taken to overcome infertility. But the throbbing womb of a loving and tender God overcomes the curse of barrenness in all its many guises.

We begin with Sarah [Sarai], wife of the patriarch Abraham [Abram]. Unable to conceive (Gen. 11:30; 16:1) and desperate to have offspring, she encouraged Abraham to have a child by her maid, Hagar. Although this was a common practice, Sarah became intensely jealous when Hagar gave birth to a boy named Ishmael, and Hagar and Ishmael were eventually sent into the wilderness. When Sarah was ninety, she was informed by three messengers of God that she was to have a child. The laughing Sarah and the incredulous Abraham, who was 100, were "granted a son," Isaac (Gen. 21:2).

Isaac, in turn, prayed to God on behalf of his wife, Rebekah, for she was unable to bear children. God "granted his prayer" (Gen. 25:21), and the twins Esau and Jacob were born. In their turn, Jacob's favorite wife, Rachel, was also unable to conceive. Jealous of her sister, Leah, who was also Jacob's wife and who had borne him four sons, Rachel pleaded with Jacob: "Give me children, or I shall die!" (Gen. 30:1). Jacob replied: "Am I in the place of God, who has withheld from you the fruit of the womb?" (30:2). Meanwhile, Leah bore two more sons. At this point, God remembered the barren Rachel, heard her, and opened her womb. Rachel's response is indicative of the biblical view of female infertility: "God has taken away my reproach" (30:23), and Joseph's birth was a sign of blessing.

For numerous other barren women, as well, God's reproach of infertility was similarly removed. Hannah, for example, wept bitterly over her affliction (1 Sam. 1:7), refused to eat, and acted as if she were in a drunken stupor before her petition was granted. Speaking out of great anxiety and vexation or distress, she pleaded:

"O LORD of hosts, if only you will look on the misery of your servant, and remember me, and not forget your servant, but will give to your servant a male child, then I will set him before you as a nazirite until the day of his death." (1 Sam. 1:11)

Manoah's wife had no children, and Elizabeth was barren and advanced in years. But God heard each of these women's anguish, and each conceived a son: After the word from an angel of the Lord, Manoah's wife gave birth to Samson (Judg. 13:2). Hannah bore Samuel, and Elizabeth had John the Baptist.

But we cannot simply celebrate with these joyous biblical stories, for that would gloss over the pain of infertility and would comply with the silence of Scripture in the face of real and unending barrenness.

Nor can we end our reading of the text with the biblical women, because there is not one woman recorded in either the Old or New Testament who, desirous of progeny, remained barren. There is not one model, mentor, or mother in Scripture with whom modern-day infertile women can connect. When a woman does not conceive, the implication from Scripture is that God does not hear her or remember her pain. A mortuary of silence engulfs the women of the empty womb as if they were attending the funeral of the unborn. The empty womb is once again a reproach, if not a curse.

The silent suffering of the infertile is punctuated with clinical treatments, surgeries, support groups, and adoption attempts. Infertile couples and individuals desiring children huddle together against what feels like God's rebuke.

A while ago, a private adoption agency with which I am familiar called a group meeting of eleven couples who had been on the agency list for several years. Some of the couples had seen each other at agency meetings. Some had shared infertility stories only to find out that they had the same specialists.

There were two agency personnel at this meeting, one with a great deal of experience, the other a new employee. The novice reviewed a list of forms that needed to be filled out in the adoptive process. One requirement involved getting police verification that the prospective adoptive parents were not criminals. A woman naively asked whether those who had never even had a parking ticket had to do this. The young agency worker, a biological mother of two, quickly remarked: "Oh, of course. We want to make sure all you adoptive couples jump through as many hoops as a biological parent."

We all winced. A biological mother surely endures many challenges, ordeals, and labor. However, for those in the agency work-up, the lists of medical tests and treatments were extensive: hysterosalpingograms, laser surgeries, high-powered medications, laparoscopies, endometrial biopsies, post-coital exams, semen analyses, ultrasounds, in-vitro fertilization (IVF), Gamete Intra-fallopian Transfer (GIFT), tuboplasty, luteal phase (LH) monitoring, temperature charts, ovulation kits. In fact, a letter from a fertility specialist was required by the agency to attest that the gamut of treatments had been depleted. Many in the adoption workshop that day felt that, in comparison to biological parents, they had already leaped through far more "hoops."

Barrenness is about grief—a miscarriage, a failed adoption, loss of fertilized embryos, unsuccessful egg retrieval, failure of implantation, ectopic pregnancy, early menopause.[1] Even without diagnostic tests, drug treatment, and the surgical procedures of infertility, a woman who fails to become pregnant dies a small death each month.

Barrenness also creates unique jealousies. When a woman undergoing infertility work-ups must wait in a clinic hallway or examining room filled with photos of babies born to patients who were successfully treated, her feelings are complicated. No barren woman resents the birth of children, but she often feels a strange resentment that one of those photos is not of her child. An unsettling envy can overtake a barren woman at family reunions, Christmas gatherings, Thanksgiving meals with relatives, class reunions—and it can be overwhelming in waiting rooms full of pregnant women. The topic of abortion can be painful because it represents a choice, an option that barren women do not have.

Barrenness is dehumanizing. From her early teens, a girl's body prepares for and reminds itself of childbearing. Women have historically had little power and often only a vague sense of control over their destiny. Infertility is the ultimate outrage: it is loss of control over one's own body, a body that plays a trick each month with false hope of future offspring.

Barrenness is depleting. The treatment procedures are physically invasive. If the clinical staff of a fertility clinic treat their patients as statistics representing success or failure, the procedures become not only intrusive but inhuman. There is no way around it. Barrenness is a curse.

Sing, O Barren One

> Sing, O barren one who did not bear;
>   burst into song and shout,
>   you who have not been in labor!
> For the children of the desolate woman will be more
>   than the children of her that is married,
>   says the LORD.
>   (Isa. 54:1)

The continuum of feelings shared by infertile men and women can be set in the context of spirituality. Jane and Jim Rhodes had waited to start a family until their education was complete. They began infertility treatments in their thirties and were eventually prompted by a nurse in the fertility clinic to consider adoption.

Jane: "When I sat in the adoption agency, waiting for the social worker, I used to stare at the two plaques on the wall:

Children are a gift from God.
Jesus Christ is Lord.

"Through the adoption process, I was glad that both statements were foremost in my mind. If I had not believed the first, I would never have subjected myself to seven years of high-powered fertility treatments. Much of that was demoralizing and degrading. Being probed and pricked in the labs, in Ultrasound, and on the examining tables made the process of conception a mere function of technology. Only the hope of having a child kept me going.

"It was the second plaque that I needed when I experienced the disappointments during the infertility work-ups. When we experienced a failed adoption while I was going through the last phases of infertility treatments, I relied on the timeless truth of the faith statement: 'Jesus Christ is Lord.' As a Christian, it was this faith understanding that gave me the ability to survive an adoption gone awry. Our social worker likened that experience to a stillbirth."

These two separate messages have sustained many prospective parents as they venture through the adoption maze. Some chapters in this book contain stories that emphasize one truth, some the other. Neither statement can stand alone. Both are essential to contain the emotions that occur during adoption.

Jane's story is of a private adoption, and through her experience, she reconsidered parallel ways of being born—most notably, being "born in the heart."

Jane: "About four years into the work-ups a nurse took the time to have what became a life-changing conversation with me. 'Have you ever considered adoption?' she asked. 'No,' I responded hastily. The nurse went on to add, 'I am adopted.' I asked her to tell me about it. My main curiosity revolved around what her adoptive parents had told her by way of explanation. She said, 'They told me I was born in their hearts,' and she went on to tell me what a wonderful life she had had, how she could not have had better parents, how much she loved them.

"The phrase 'born in their hearts' became a pivotal image in my life. Born in the heart. I had never thought of anything other than biological birth. Since that transforming conversation, I have lived it—over and over again.

"I once stood on the banks of the River Seine with a biological mother who had lost her eleven-year-old daughter to cancer. She reminisced about the day her little elementary-school daughter had gone on a school outing on a chartered boat. As we stood at the dock, I who was childless, felt for a moment the depths of a mother's grief. It was then I saw how a child is carried in the heart.

"Biological mothers carry a child in their uterus and also in their heart. Many adoptive mothers do not know what it feels like to have a baby move in their belly, although adoptive mothers who have suffered miscarriages or birthed children through labor would know. Those of us who do not know, I believe, develop other sensitivities; one of these is to understand the intricacies of 'being born and carried in the heart.'

Mighty Wrestlings

Then Rachel said, "With mighty wrestlings I have wrestled with my sister, and have prevailed." (Gen. 30:8)

There are four insights I would like to give to those involved in any way in the adoption process: relatives, ministers, and friends, as well as parents. Adoption, like surrogate parenting in the story of Rachel, Jacob, and the birth mother Bilhah, has its own set of "mighty wrestlings." In the competition between Rachel and Leah to bear sons to Jacob, both used their servants (Bilhah and Zilpah) to bear sons for Jacob. Rachel instructed Jacob to have intercourse with her servant Bilhah "that she may bear upon my knees and that I too may have children through her" (Gen. 30:3).

First, like Rachel and Bilhah, there can be a powerful bond of connectedness between the adoptive parents and the birth parents. There is a unique if not mystical connectedness, even if they have never met. In contemporary culture, there is often an exchange of letters and gifts. One birth mother wrote her son a simple and profoundly loving letter, speaking of her love for her son and her desire to give him a better life. This note became a priceless keepsake that the adoptive parents shall give to their son someday. Although lawyers and the closed adoption process kept adoptive and birth parents apart, the adoptive mother decided to send the birth mother a string of pearls as a graduation gift. After all, she had given the "pearl of great value" (Matt. 13:46), her son.

Second, adoption and surrogate parenting call forth a range of emotions, pain as well as elation. Just as in the Biblical story of Rachel, there is anger, jealousy, and stress as well as elation and fulfillment. For example, two friends were driving in California, where one lived and the other was attending a conference. The biological mother, resident of California, pointed out the hospital where her only son was born. She said with great affection, "My son, Tom, was born in that hospital." She recalled a certain room, a set of nurses. It was a very happy memory. Her friend, an adoptive mom, had a different set of memories. She remembered driving up late to a Catholic hospital in another town after the lawyer called to say a baby boy had been born. She waited until the birth mother had had the chance to see the baby twice and had taken her time to leave the hospital. In the darkness, she stood outside the multistoried, concrete hospital and gazed upward at the lit rooms: "Somewhere on one of those floors, in some crib, is my son." In the infant nursery lay a living, active being who would alter the course of her life. For that hospital, she had happy associations.

Recollections of another hospital only brought pain, however. Twins were born to her, or so she thought, as she stood behind the glass in the delivery room and watched twin girls enter the world by Caesarean section. She visited the babies, took gifts to the birth mother, and helped name the girls. She still remembered—now with pain—calling her parents from the pay phone: "We have twin daughters, mother and dad." She remembered the celebratory meal with the hospital chaplain, the same chaplain who would be with her in the agony to follow. The birth mother changed her mind.

She remembered when the fertility process was closed for her. She thought of the hospital where her fertilized embryos had lived for a while and failed to implant, the closest she had gotten to the birth experience. She wept over the death of her unborn children.

Third, loved ones in their ignorance can say hurtful things to infertile and adoptive couples. In the Bible, Jacob reacted in anger to Rachel. In our contemporary culture, here is a modern example of insensitivity. A couple adopted after years of infertility. There had been family pressure on this couple because the wife's parents had no grandsons. A plaque was strategically placed in the home; it stated, "What every family needs is a grandfather." The adoptive grandfather poked his head into the baby's room, gazed at his adopted grandson, and said to the daughter: "Now, maybe you'll have one of your own." Welling inside of the adoptive mom, amid the hurt, was the feeling, 'He is my own." Later, many people visited this baby and told her stories of friends who had adopted, shortly thereafter become pregnant, and had their *own* children.

Fourth, the emotional and physical bonding process beyond parenting a child may take a while, as it sometimes also does with biological children. Adoption does not necessarily evoke instant love.

How do you know when you are ready to adopt? I would respond: let the idea gestate in you for a while. Putting yourself on a list with an agency or contacting a lawyer does not mean you will adopt quickly. You will have ample time for doubts, for confirmation, for practical preparation like a baby-care course.

The theological underpinnings of adoption helped me become ready. When I realized I was adopted as a child of God into God's household of faith, I had the biblical basis I needed for the actual practice or praxis of adoption. In other words, when I saw adoption as a paradigm for the life of a Christian, when I really grasped the concept of "being born in the heart," I became ready. I became "expectant."

The Fruitless Tree

Rachel was under a great deal of familial pressure. The biblical family tree was dependent on the descendants or "seed" of Abraham, Isaac, and Jacob. "I will multiply thy seed exceedingly" promises Yahweh (Gen. 16:10, KJV) on numerous occasions (Exod. 32:13; Josh. 24:3; 2 Sam. 7:12; 1 Chr. 17:11, and so forth). The "seed" of Israel needed continually to be sown to perpetuate the promises of God.

Barrenness was not only a curse for the matriarchs, the women. It was a loss of immortality for the patriarchs, the male lineage. A barren patriarch would be like a tree yielding no fruit. Christ came of the seed of David (John 7:42). Paul identified himself as an Israelite, of the seed of Abraham (Rom. 11:1). Jewish scholar Jon Levenson suggests that "generational continuity" or the birth of offspring is, for Jews, the equivalent of life after death, for the Hebrew Bible has no doctrine of the resurrection of the dead. For Jews, death is tragic, final, and universal. In the book of Genesis, he says, "infertility and the loss of children (which have connections to famine and exile) are the rough functional equivalent of death, and miraculous birth is the functional equivalent of resurrection."[2]

"In Judaism, biology is everything," states Michael Gold, Rabbi of Beth El Congregation in Pittsburgh, Pennsylvania. He traces the emphasis in Jewish law on bloodlines, biology, and pure lineage to the days of Ezra and the return from the Babylonian exile.[3] Gold's two adopted children have a Gentile birth mother, and their biological heritage affects their religious status. Although Gold and his wife adopted them as infants, raised them in a traditional Jewish home, and encouraged them to convert to Judaism, their bloodline means the children are restricted to a certain class.[4]

Gold, as an adoptive parent, regards the book of Ruth as the most dramatic and hopeful instance of Judaism's lack of concern with biological heritage.[5] Ruth, a Moabite, not an Israelite, married a Hebrew man. She was widowed and chose to return to Judah with her mother-in-law, Naomi. Ruth chose to belong to her husband's people, the Israelites or Hebrews, and she later married Boaz, a Hebrew. Whereas the Torah stated that no Moabite could be admitted into the Assembly of the Lord (Deut. 23:4), Ruth, a Moabite, becomes King David's great-grandmother. Jesus Christ is of the genealogy of David, son of Abraham (Matt. 1:1). Does Ruth, adopted into the family tree, challenge that tree?[6]

Although there is no specific word for adoption in the Old Testament, there are prominent instances of fosterage or legitimization (taking a child as son), which resemble adoption. Moses, for example, became the son of Pharoah's daughter (Exod. 2:10). Genubath was reared by Tahpenes among the sons of Pharaoh (1 Kgs. 11:14–20). Esther was taken in by her uncle Mordecai (Esth. 2:7, 15). Michal was childless, but was considered the "mother" of her five nephews (2 Sam. 6:23). Joseph takes sons of Jacob—Ephraim, Manasseh, Reuben, and Simeon—as his own (Gen. 48:5–6).

Does the tree of life in Judaism become fruitful through the practice of taking a child into the family, whether we call this practice adoption or legitimization or fosterage? In Israel, would this child be considered "seed" or a part of the tree of life? According to one scholar, the importance of the continuance of the *seed of the man* through a son is determinative of adoptive status. In other words, it seems that adoption is only legitimate when a male child is needed to continue "the seed."[7] The story of Esther, a Hebrew woman, adopted by her uncle Mordecai after her parents died, challenges this theory, however. Through Esther's marriage to King Ahasuerus, a Gentile, the Jews in Persia were saved from slaughter. This is not the traditional way to preserve the Hebrew family lineage or tree. Yet Esther, a woman, continues the seed and prevents a branch of the Hebrew tree from becoming fruitless and extinct.

During the time the New Testament was written, the royal Roman family tree faced the threat of extinction. The Julio-Claudian dynasty that ruled Rome was concerned with perpetuating its lineage. These emperors ruled as Divine Father of the Holy Roman Empire, and they needed royal sons—by birth or adoption—to continue the family rule and specifically to continue the power of the father (*patria potestas*). In the Roman Empire, the entire household was under the authority of the father.

Adoption became critical to continuing the lineage of the Julio-Claudian emperors:

Octavius (Augustus)	27 B.C.E.–14 C.E.
Tiberius	14 C.E.–37 C.E.
Gaius (Caligula)	37 C.E.–41 C.E.
Claudius	41 C.E.–54 C.E.
Nero	54 C.E.–68 C.E.

Julius Caesar adopted his grandnephew Octavius as his son in 44 B.C.E. After Julius Caesar's assassination, he was deified or considered a god. When Julius Caesar was deified, Octavius became "the son of a god."[8]

Octavius was the first of the Julio-Claudian emperors. He was the emperor when Christ was born. The title "Augustus," meaning "reverend," was bestowed on him in 27 B.C.E. by the senate, which elevated him above the state.[9] The Lukan account of Jesus' birth reads:

> In those days a decree went out from Emperor Augustus [Octavius] that all the world should be registered. (Luke 2:1)

Augustus in turn had no sons by either of his wives, but by his first wife he had a daughter, Julia. He adopted two of his three grandsons, but both died young. He then forced the forty-six-year-old Tiberius to divorce the wife Tiberius loved and marry Julia, Augustus's daughter. Augustus then adopted his new son-in-law as his son.

Tiberius had one biological son and one adopted son, Germanicus. When both died before him, Tiberius adopted Gaius Caligula, the son of his own adopted son Germanicus, as his grandson to be successor. Caligula, in turn, adopted his cousin, the young Tiberius, but he died before Caligula. When Caligula died with neither descendant nor brother, his uncle Claudius was designated as emperor. In turn, Claudius adopted his stepson Nero, the son of his second wife Agrippine.

Clearly, during Christ's lifetime and after his death, the legal and political acceptance and ramifications of adoption were played out at the highest level of Roman government, as emperors who had no biological sons chose heirs to ensure the continuation of the Julio-Claudian family tree. For Christians, this becomes extremely significant because the three New Testament books that mention adoption—Galatians (ca. 55 C.E.), Ephesians (ca. 58–63 C.E.), and Romans (54–58 C.E.)—were written during a time when adoption secured the lineage of the ruling family in Rome. The writer of these three books is generally taken to be Paul or from the school of Paul. Paul, who might have been a Roman citizen, (Acts 16:37; 22:25–29), would have been aware, in any case, of the process that secured the so-called "divine ancestry" of emperors. And so the writer of Ephesians, Galatians, and Romans developed "the divine ancestry of the sons of God" through Christ, sons secured through adoption, (Eph. 1:5).

Jesus too chose heirs to ensure the survival of his family, but his lineage is not of flesh and blood. The language of Ephesians introduces the idea of a Divine Father, patria potestas [power of the father], inheritance, and lineage (see chapter 8). Jesus configures a spiritual family or household. It is noteworthy that at the end of Jesus' life, he used words that constructed a new familial relationship among those closest to him. To his biological mother Mary who stood at the foot of the cross and to his beloved disciple John, he spoke in the language of family or household of faith: "Woman [Mary], behold your son!" To John: "Behold your mother!" Early in Jesus' ministry, when approached by his biological family, he had confounded the crowds by his query in which he seemed to deny this family: Who are my mother and brothers? In parallel fashion, at the conclusion of his earthly ministry, he points to an even higher level of relatedness. This greater reality of the household of faith is created by a spiritual birth out of the womb-love or the compassion of God.

Chapter 3

Conception in the Barren Places

> **Sam Cesaretti:** *"I no longer think God speaks to us from the barren places of our lives only. I have come to think, rather simply, that it is from the barren places of our lives that we hear God most clearly."*

*P*eople generally think of conception as the act of becoming pregnant. Couples can often name both the place and occasion they conceived a child. For adoptive parents, conception occurs when an idea about adoption originates and forms in their minds and souls. This conceiving of the idea is followed by a gestation period, a time in which the idea of adopting is carried in the mind.

In the twenty-first century, barren places often accompany or follow singleness, infertility, a hysterectomy, a miscarriage, a vasectomy, the loss of a child, the realization that one's childbearing years and possibilities are over. Jane Rhodes speaks of the conception of the idea of adoption, which occurred for her in a barren or childless place:

Jane: "When you ask me when I *conceived* of the idea of adopting a daughter, I cannot pinpoint a time, a moment, a month. I used to walk the beach saying, 'I know I have a daughter somewhere.' I both yearned for a daughter and realized that God was working even through the agony of the infertility treatments we continued."

Jane speaks of *conception* as a religious awareness that she was to have a child. She anticipated this blessed event; she carried the idea of her adopted child within herself. The process, like pregnancy, was not without its risks, and they illustrate Jane's understanding of how this child was meant for her:

Jane: "A child was born seven weeks early and stayed four weeks in a neonatal intensive care unit. She weighed two pounds and fourteen ounces. The birth mother had been in touch with a lawyer who represented a couple waiting to adopt this baby. However, when she entered this world as a pre-emie, the couple backed away. The birth mother tried to reach the lawyer from the hospital, to no avail, and she was left without a plan.

"After the baby girl was released from the hospital, the birth mother accompanied her father on a business trip to a distant state. They brought with them the tiny baby, now six pounds. Upon arrival, the birth mother thumbed through the Yellow Pages. She chose an agency—ours. The social worker drove to her and showed her portfolios. She chose us. We had been waiting six years with this agency; we had experienced two failed adoptions, both girls. When I drove two hours with the social worker to pick up our daughter, I had many feelings, but from the first moment I saw her, I loved her. The bonding was instantaneous.

"When did I conceive of this daughter? It has been such a long process. In some ways, I really do believe that God conceives of us, knowing us in the mother's womb, knowing us even before we are formed in the womb. So conception for me meant relying on a process in which my daughter and I were matched. I did my share of trying to find her, though. She is almost two. I never tire of touching her baby cheeks, of watching the wonder in her eyes. I am awed still at her coming. For me, adoption was the gift conceived amid the grief of infertility and in the barren places."

Linda and Harry Turnbull, after several unsuccessful surgeries, felt they had reached the end of the road and determined to reconcile themselves to a life without children. However, an opportune comment started the conception of an adoption that led to the placement of a child in their home.

Linda: "We met some friends who had used the agency that we finally used. One of them, who had had a horrible experience with international adoption, looked me in the eye and said: 'But it would work for you.' Harry and I discussed whether we could possibly go through a disappointment. This is probably the last chance, we thought. . . . Something clearly happened when my friend looked me in the eye and said, 'It would work for you.' We kept taking the steps. Things happened quickly over a period of six months.

"We could have let that comment drop. But there was something happening that sort of led us on toward our son. . . . I can't possibly imagine things ever being any other way, or him not being our son."

Childlessness

One out of five couples today find themselves in the barren places of infertility and childlessness. However, some of these same couples and growing numbers of singles are later finding themselves "in the family way" through adoption.

> Most noticeable in recent years is the increase in transracial and transcultural adoptions, usually white parents adopting foreign-born or minority American children. Sociologists cite two primary factors behind this trend, factors that are likely to continue: the first is unavailability of healthy white infants as more white, unwed mothers keep their babies; and second, a new type of adoptive parent—single or married, with or without biological children—who adopts for religious, social, or humanitarian reasons.[1]

Not all of those who choose to adopt must deal with the barren places of infertility. Some have had biological children first, and then for a variety of reasons expand their families through adoption. However, more often than not, a prospective adoptive parent will have dealt with infertility and/or miscarriage. When a couple or a single woman opts for infertility treatments, the inability to conceive biologically can create not only a sense of personal failure but also one of being cursed by God. Bruce Rappaport, author of *The Open Adoption Book*, comments:

> In some ways, we have not come far from the days when childless couples were labelled barren, cursed by God. Infertility is often correlated with sexually transmitted diseases or a Yuppie life-style of self-indulgence. Whatever the specific explanation, infertility is usually seen as the couple's own fault.[2]

It is in these barren places of infertility, miscarriage, and childlessness that many couples and singles turn to Scripture. There they encounter the seven barren matriarchs: Sarah, Rebecca, Rachel, Leah, the wife of Manoah, Hannah, and Zion as mother. As I noted, they receive no comfort, for barrenness in the Bible is seen as a curse and a humiliation. In fact, Sheol or hell is likened to a barren womb (Prov. 30:16). Fertility is a sign of and reward for faithfulness, prayer, obedience. The biblical barren-women-made-fertile is a sign of answered prayer, of the elevation of the humble, and of the world to come.[3]

How is a barren woman in the twenty-first century to identify with any of the barren matriarchs in Scripture, all of whom became fertile? Should she, instead, identify with Tamar or Jephthah's daughter, who never conceived? The fact that Tamar was raped by Amnon and left to lead a desolate life, the fact that Jephthah's daughter was offered as a burnt offering after her father's foolish vow, makes such identification painfully problematic. Nor is it easy for barren men of the twenty-first century to identify with Scripture, because all the biblical patriarchs eventually are "blessed" with biological children through their wives.

We will, however, find modern stories of faith, in which modern matriarchs and patriarchs of the church speak of other ways of blessing.

Modern Matriarchs

Theresa

As she stood on a bridge in Cambridge, England, Theresa Russell felt the first flicker of certainty: I am going to have a baby. She meant a biological child. She had been pregnant once in her first marriage, but miscarried. On her forty-first birthday, she opened her Bible to 2 Kgs. 4:8–37, the passage about the Shunammite woman who was granted a son in her old age. Theresa continued to imagine a biological child as she proceeded through infertility work-ups while in seminary, studying to become a minister. Doctors discovered and removed an ovarian cyst, a tumor, adhesions, and uterine fibroids. Following surgery, the surgeon optimistically forecast: "You will now be able to have a baby."

That was Friday. On the following Tuesday, Theresa and her husband Mike learned that the pathology report had revealed borderline cancer, and a hysterectomy was recommended. That same evening, the physician asked if they would consider adoption. Theresa describes this as a broken moment, as if time had been ruptured. "We said, 'Yes,' but we were numb."

She read Isa. 54:1: "Sing, O barren one who did not bear, burst into song and shout, you who have not been in labor!" Theresa, in seminary at the time, took this as God's assurance that she would be able to nurture children in a future ministry. Two months after her hysterectomy, in January 1991, the phone rang. A nurse from her obstetrician's office spoke: "I know you think this is going to be a terrible year. We're at war. You're still recovering from that awful surgery. But it's not going to be a bad year. We have a baby." The nurse meant that a woman several months pregnant was making plans through that doctor's office to place her baby through adoption. This expectant woman had chosen Theresa and Mike.

Months later, unaware that this young woman had entered the hospital in labor, Theresa read Ruth 1:16: "Your people shall be my people." Later that day, a daughter was born. With a new perception of blended families, shaped in part by Ruth's story, Theresa remarked, "God does provide for one people to accept another as their own." Ruth had been so accepted, and that became one biblical anchor to Theresa's hope.

Theresa and Mike received their baby. By state law, the birth mother had ten days in which to change her mind. During those days, as Theresa and Mike kept the baby in their home, Mike left for work each morning saying to his daughter, "Will you be here when I come home?" As they watched the newborn, Theresa wondered if God watched her with equal absorption. Did God as Parent gaze on her with such delight? In all her moments of disappointment in infertility, Theresa articulated her belief: "The ultimate foundation has to be that 'God is,' even in chaos when things feel out of control."

For Theresa, adoption became "a way of having a baby." Although her joy was and is still predominant, she remembers her fears. "I was so afraid, so unsure of how adoption works, how it comes together. . . . There is a basic instinct, at least for me, that really wanted a child, yet part of me was scared to death. It's like now going into ministry. I'm so excited . . . yet I'm scared to death." She likens the uncertainties of entering ministry to her fears surrounding adoption. And she likens the fears and anxiety in adoption to those in pregnancy. "You have to allow the process to happen. . . . Adoption can't be much different from a pregnancy, it just can't be." Amid the fears, the desire to have a child prevails, and joy triumphs.

Susan

Susan Hall, a single, professional woman, made up her mind, at age thirty-four, that she would have a child by age thirty-six. She tried for several months to conceive through artificial insemination. Then, she decided to become a mother through adoption. "I had prayed a lot," she says, "that I would get the right child for me, that God would find—somewhere in the world—*the* right child for me, who needed *me* as a mother as I needed that child as a child. I had a real strong belief in the match. I started bonding then."

One day, Susan was given a picture of a three-year-old girl in Chile, and from the picture became totally committed to that child. "I already considered that one my child. In a sense, if the adoption had fallen through, in the same way people have miscarriages or give up their children for adoption, I would have still thought about that child every year on her birthday, wondering where she was."

At various points, the adoption seemed doubtful, and Susan shed tears of anguish. She even asked the agency social worker, in the event that "her child" was placed with another family, to place the child in another state. To run into "her child" at a parents' support group would be too painful.

Susan's story is filled with clerks, lawyers, judges, foster mother, and translators. Eventually, the call came to go to South America. When she saw her little girl for the first time, she burst into tears. "That was the culmination of everything. I imagine it is like that when babies are born. I cried for a long time. The Chilean translator, foster mother, and lawyer all just sat around looking at me." Finally, Susan asked the translator to tell the lawyer she was happy.

Susan took the three-year-old to a hotel and began her song of joy. "I was fascinated. It is sort of like when people have babies, and they count toes and fingers. I was fascinated that she could do a puzzle; she was an actual person to me now." Her daughter enjoyed room service and ate voraciously, but balked at a bath and a change of clothes. To calm her screaming child, Susan carried her back and forth in the hotel room. A song burst forth as the tired, new mother paced the floor. Her song of joy in the warm climate of South America was "Chestnuts Roasting on an Open Fire."

Songs of Joy

It is through Scripture's songs of joy that barren women like Susan and Theresa can relate to the matriarchs of Scripture. The best-known song of joy, the Magnificat, was sung by Mary, mother of Jesus (Luke 1:46–55). Hannah's song of elation (1 Sam. 2:1–10) is less familiar to us, but it, too, celebrates the divine gift of life. Both songs testify to God's great reversal: God exalts those of low degree.

The motif of the barren woman, central to both early Christian reflection and rabbinic midrashim,[4] taught people something about the way God is and works. The barren matriarchs functioned to show that the gift of life came from God alone and that God could overcome obstacles. As scholar Mary Calloway has noted, "The Yahwist presupposed that any dreadful state, no matter how irredeemable in human eyes, could be used by Yahweh in the fulfillment of his promise. Not only could he, but Yahweh seemed to prefer working through those who were least likely and least able to do what he needed. . . . The stories of the barren matriarchs are primary examples of Yahweh's use of evil for good."[5]

The story of Hannah, the childless wife of Elkanah, illustrates God's stance toward the suffering, the tormented, the humiliated, the poor. Hannah was tormented by Peninnah, Elkanah's other wife who had borne him children, because "the LORD had closed her [Hannah's] womb" (1 Sam. 1:5). Hannah wept and could not eat. She petitioned God and prayed as if in a trance. God granted Hannah her petition; she became pregnant and gave birth to Samuel, dedicating him to God, as she had promised. The barren Hannah was an example of the *anawim* (the poor of Yahweh), and the reversal of her situation became an example of God raising the humble and answering prayer.

After Samuel's birth and dedication back to God, Hannah burst forth in a prayerful song of exultation (1 Sam. 2:1–10) that underscores the great reversals of God: the poor are made rich, the lowly are exalted, the barren become fertile, the hungry are full, the feeble become strong.

> "My heart exults in the LORD,
>   my strength is exalted in my God. . . .
> The barren has borne seven,
>   but she who has many children is forlorn.
> The LORD kills and brings to life;
>   [the LORD] brings down to Sheol and raises up.
> The LORD makes poor and makes rich;
>   [The LORD] brings low, [the LORD] also exalts.
> [The LORD] raises up the poor from the dust."
>
> (1 Sam. 2:1, 5b–8)

Both Hannah's song and Mary's Magnificat connect barrenness and blessing, childlessness and the divine gift of conception, God reversing the plight of the lowly or infertile. Mary's song of exuberance also speaks of another reversal: God exalts those of low degree. Mary, a peasant woman, was to bear the Son of God. Hannah, lowly through her barrenness, was also to experience a reversal, from infertile to fertile, from shame to fulfillment.

Hannah's story is a *hinge* story. By this, I mean that the focus of the story pivots away from the woman as individual to the woman as symbol or paradigm for the experience of Israel.[6] According to Mary Calloway, the experience of Israel is symbolized by the city of Zion or Jerusalem, depicted at times as a barren mother, a desolate woman (Isa. 54:1). Jerusalem as the mother in mourning is based on the description of Rachel weeping for her children (Jer. 31:15).

The barren matriarch stories can be taken to include physical and spiritual conception. In the following verses, Jerusalem or Zion is described as being in labor and giving birth:

> Before she was in labor
>   she gave birth;
> before her pain came upon her
>   she delivered a son. . . .

Yet as soon as Zion was in labor
   she delivered her children.
Shall I open the womb and not deliver?
   says the LORD.
shall I, the one who delivers, shut the womb?
   says your God.
Rejoice with Jerusalem, and be glad for her,
   all you who love her;
rejoice with her in joy,
   all you who mourn over her—
that you may nurse and be satisfied
   from her consoling breast;
that you may drink deeply with delight
   from her glorious bosom. . . .
and you shall nurse and be carried on her arm,
and dandled on her knees.
As a mother comforts her child,
   so I will comfort you;
   you shall be comforted in Jerusalem.
             (Isa. 66:7, 8b–11, 12b–13)

Gentiles are not the "natural" sons or children of "mother" Jerusalem or of Zion. The birth of the Christian community has been seen as a fulfillment of the prophecy in Isa. 54:1–3: "Sing, O barren one who did not bear . . . your descendants will possess the nations."[7] In the book of Galatians, the adoption imagery is used to depict the coming of Gentiles into the family of faith through the barren mother Jerusalem (Zion). The biblical mechanism of adoption will be discussed at length in chapter 8.

Ephesians portrays the son of the virgin Mary as firstborn of a new family into which all others come through adoption. In this way, Mary as matriarch of the church connects the line of biblical barren matriarchs (and their sons) with today's barren women to whom a child is given. And in turn, contemporary barren women claim God's promises to be faithful and to hear their cries. Their adopted children stand as symbols of God's grace, of God's favor, of God's hearing their prayers.

In the voices of some contemporary barren women, we hear echoes of the biblical matriarchs. Just as Hannah promised to give her child to God in service:

"For this child I prayed; and the LORD has granted me the petition that I made to him. Therefore I have lent him to the LORD; as long as he lives, he is given to the LORD." (1 Sam. 1:27–28) so the words of biological and adoptive mother Alicia Fox today:

> God has given them [the children] to me to raise, and that's a gift. . . . The
> best thing that I can do is to raise them to give them back to God so they
> can go on their way. I hope I can do it.

As contemporary adoptive matriarchs and patriarchs will confirm, there are differing ways of "conceiving" a child. When I first began writing this book a decade ago, I devised the chapters to parallel and replicate the biological process and stages of a child coming into the family: conception, expectant waiting, homecoming, first days home. However, I now know these phases are quite different. Thus, while keeping the chapter titles intact, I have reworked the pages to reflect an acceptance-of-differences between a biologically constructed family and one designed through adoption. It would be dishonest to deny the dissimilarities that exist in terms of process. It would be equally deceptive to deny the essence of parenting, to fail to acknowledge the love I have encountered in the interviews with adoptive parents. They know that the essence of mothering and fathering is the same no matter how they "were with child."

Alicia, who is both a biological and adoptive mother, addresses the essence of mothering: "I am grateful," she says, "that I had the opportunity to have the experience of actually giving birth. But it's very clear to me now that giving birth is a biological thing, and being a mother is something totally different. I am as much my adopted son Steve's mother as I am my biological daughter Elizabeth's. If you were to take him away from me, I would die. If you were to take Elizabeth away from me, I would die, so the bonding is complete. There's no doubt. These are my two children . . . I thank God every day for the chance to raise two children."

This feeling is common. Another mother has written to sociologist H. David Kirk, expressing her love for both her biological son Johnny and her adopted son Richard, who died. The adoption occurred after she'd had several miscarriages and a stillbirth. She was answering the question: Can I love a life that is not of my blood? "Richard came to us when he was a few days old," she wrote, "a lovable little one with the most beautiful round blue eyes. . . . I cared for him as I had for Johnny and nature did the rest. After his death (at less than a year), I often thought, one doesn't love their husband or wife upon first meeting but one grows in love as each shares. To me the same is true of an adopted child, for if it had been Johnny that was taken, the pain could not have been any more severe."[8]

Modern Patriarchs

As we noted in chapter 2, the barren patriarchs and matriarchs in Scripture found ways to have children. Abram had a son by Sarai's maid, Hagar, long before Sarai knew that she would conceive. When Rachel "saw that she bore Jacob no children" (Gen. 30:1), she gave him her maid Bilhah, who bore Jacob a son. The implications of having no male heir were so devastating that the patriarchs found ways to continue their line.

Tom and Darcy

Although the times are different, contemporary America is replete with examples of "barren patriarchs." Tom Algood and his wife Darcy, a biracial couple, had three biological children and then applied to adopt through their state's Department of Human Resources.

Tom yearned for another child. "Not having the experience of giving birth to children," he said, "all I could do was sit and wait, and be patient." From the time he was accepted as an adoptive father by the agency to the moment he received son Carl, his experience was like a pregnancy to him. Tom's emotions during the adoption were the same he'd felt during Darcy's pregnancies. He describes the man's role in pregnancy as waiting and supporting. "Getting approved by an agency is like finding out you're pregnant." For Tom, the only difference was the uncertainty of the onset of labor. "When you do finally get the phone call, and when you do meet the baby for the first time . . . the feeling is probably pretty much the same. . . . I was convinced this was the child God wanted us to have, so I had no problem relating to Carl as our son."

When asked how and when he conceived of the idea of adoption, he answered that the yearning for another child came some years after he'd had a vasectomy. He and Darcy were not able to afford a vasectomy reversal, a procedure not covered by their insurance. They then contacted the state, requesting a biracial child. Asked when he first felt that Carl was his son, Tom answered, "The first time I saw him in the office [of the social worker]." The agency asked that Tom and Darcy spend a few hours with the baby in a motel room to get acquainted and make their final decision: "He [the baby] grabbed ahold of my beard and wouldn't let go. . . . I take care of the babies at my church . . . I know I have bonded with the kids when they get ahold of my beard and don't want to let go. . . . Once he [the baby] grabbed ahold of my beard, I knew everything would be fine."

Conception is generally defined as the act of becoming pregnant through the union of sperm and egg. Conception is also the origin of an idea. Darcy remembered that during their engagement period, she and Tom had decided to have three children and adopt one. She added, "This was a concept that we were already accepting into our lifestyle as a matter of course." When Darcy and Tom did adopt, she did everything she could to "re-create the pregnancy" out of a suspicion that their baby had not been held much in the foster home. Darcy carried him everywhere in a snuggly, rocked him, breastfed him. "We were really into attachment-style parenting, and we believe in fostering deep emotional ties. . . . The only other thing I would like to add is that during the 'pregnancy stage,' we went through a lot of emotional ups and downs in waiting for this baby. We wanted to get it over with and get the baby. One technique I developed to calm my urgency was a little prayer. I used to talk to God a lot about this baby . . . I would ask God to bless every pregnant woman . . . When we pray for ourselves when we are pregnant, we pay attention to what we do and how we feel. I didn't want to miss that experience with the 'adopted pregnancy.' I just began to ask God to bless every pregnant woman I saw. It could have been any pregnant woman out there carrying my future child. . . . After a while, I began to pray, 'Lord, just let us be the answer to this woman's prayer.' We figured that somewhere a woman was making a decision to give up her child."

Conception may be the origin of an idea in the mind of God. Tom had his own thoughts on this subject of conception: "Our son knows he is adopted. He understands that he did not have to come out of Darcy's womb to be our son. It is God's decision that he was our son, and he picked us, and we picked him. That makes it a bit more special. I knew he picked me out when he grabbed ahold of my beard in the motel room. He hung onto it, and he's been playing with it ever since."

Sam and Peggy

Like Abraham and Sarah, Sam Cesaretti and his wife Peggy tried for years to get pregnant. Going through the infertility work ups were "agonizing" and "humiliating" for Sam. At the point of in vitro fertilization, the couple decided not to continue the medical treatments. They started thinking about adoption soon after that, beginning what became a complicated process. They opted for international adoption and were on a waiting list for a child in Paraguay when that country closed its borders to adoption. They started over, completed new forms, waited, and were next in line for an adoption in Colombia, South America. Sam was rejected by a Catholic orphanage because of his status as Protestant minister—an unusual rejection, but the orphanage personnel were nervous in the wake of scandals concerning American televangelists. Sam appealed the decision, but his appeal was denied.

Next, they tried Peru, and received word in November, 1990, that there was a child. They named him Adam: "we got word . . . and went down there Christmas Day, 1990. There was a little baby, his name was Jesus. We originally wanted to keep his name but decided in this culture to have a little boy named Jesus who is picked up on Christmas day, born to an unwed pregnant teenager in a poor country, that would have been a little too much for him."

Sam and Peggy stayed in Peru for ten weeks, a period they describe as "emotional chaos." Sam said, "It was the most emotional, agonizing experience of my life. I'd been in Nicaragua in the Contra War, and I'd spent a month in the Soviet Union. But this was just as emotionally turbulent as can be." The waiting periods, the bribery, the slow process, the complications with Peruvian government officials made for extraordinary emotional highs and lows. But through it, Sam bonded intensely with his infant, a child whose arrival was long overdue.

For Sam and Peggy, the conception of an adopted child occurred not only through barren places of their lives, but in the turbulent spaces: "We know how precarious life is, how fragile it is, and how hard it is to come by." In the ten weeks of waiting in Peru, when the adoption was in disarray, Sam experienced more profoundly what he had often preached: reliance on the sovereignty of God. And at his son's baptism, he was asked to affirm the belief that children are not our own. After all that he had been through in the "conception" process, he wanted to shout, "This kid is mine." At the same time, Sam realized, "It was the most freeing experience I've ever had to realize there's a God who doesn't desire for this little kid's hairs to be harmed and whose arms are so much sturdier than the shaky arms of this father."

In a subsequent Lenten sermon in 1993, titled "Is There Life After Barrenness?", Sam concluded:

> Barrenness, even today, can be excruciating. One rejoices at each birth of a friend's baby, but one wonders, "Why not us?" Nowadays there are various options that bring hope to a barren couple . . . in vitro fertilization, surrogate mothering. Some have even been known to go down to foreign lands for months and spend their life's savings to have a child.
>
> But there were no such options for Abraham and Sarah. They were barren. They had no foreseeable future. Barrenness in the Bible does not just mean an empty womb; it is a symbol for the hopelessness of humanity.
>
> But barrenness also became the arena of God's life-giving action.

"Move," God says [to Abraham and Sarah]. "Go to my promise. I will bless you and make of you a blessing."

I no longer think God speaks to us from the barren places of our lives only. I have come to think, rather, simply that it is from the barren places of our lives that we hear God most clearly.

Chapter 4

Expectant Waiting

We know that the whole creation has been groaning in labor pains until now; and not only the creation, but we ourselves, who have the first fruits of the Spirit, groan inwardly while we wait for adoption.
(Rom. 8:22–23)

In the Family Way

"I'm expecting," says the pregnant woman. Immediately, we know that she is carrying a baby in her womb. The pregnant woman's body and emotions adjust gradually to the new life inside her. She feels the baby kicking, moving, turning. She may have seen an ultrasound, perhaps indicating the gender of the baby. The bonding process between mother and child begins before the baby is born. Usually, the pregnant mother has eight or nine months to prepare a place for the "new arrival." What does it mean for a prospective adoptive parent to be expectant, anxiously awaiting the birth or arrival of her or his child? Is there a parallel preparation process in adoption?

I mentioned earlier that a healthy adoptive family learns to accept the differences between themselves and a non-adoptive family. While there are obvious dissimilarities in the way a child comes into each of these families, there is a parallel in the course of waiting, marking time for the new arrival.

Expectant waiting is the anticipation of a child coming home, coming into the family. It can be filled with moments of gladness or, sometimes, if the adoption miscarries, grief. It can be an anxious yet joyful period. Expectant waiting involves risk, not only in the anticipatory phase before the placement of a child, but often in the waiting period after the placement and before the adoption is legal. Waiting periods to finalize an adoption vary from state to state. Researchers on adoption are attempting to help families with the conflicting adoption statutes.[1] According to the data assembled by Adam Pertman, author of *Adoption Nation* and an adoptive parent, about half of the states prohibit a pregnant woman from signing relinquishment papers before her child is born. However, states differ as to how long after the birth a mother must wait, with the time ranging from twelve hours to fifteen days. There is also a period of time in which birth parents can revoke their consent to relinquish, and state law also varies on the length of the revocation period. In addition, when children are adopted across state lines, adopting parents must comply with the Interstate Compact on the Placement of Children, which, according to Pertman, "is so bureaucratically and inconsistently administered that it often hinders rather than expedites the process."[2] In international adoptions, the countries involved—China, Romania, and Russia, for example—keep changing adoption regulations.

Each birth mother and each birth father has her or his own version of the delivery and birth of their child. Surely, no two accounts are the same. It is important that each birth parent tell her/his own story. It is equally important to value the stories of adoptive parents, for there are no identical experiences in this complicated process. A few examples will illustrate the range of emotions and experiences in expectant waiting.

"We are expecting a call any day from the agency, now that the home study is completed," says the prospective adoptive parent. A *home study* is an on-site visit(s) to the future home of the adoptee; it is usually conducted by a social worker employed or hired by an adoption agency or the Department of Human Services. It involves paperwork, questionnaires, interviews with the prospective parents, criminal background checks, fingerprinting, and the payment of a fee. The idea of being evaluated as "fit parents" can be disquieting.

For those adopting, expectant waiting can begin with the first call to an agency or a lawyer and can last many years. With an agency, there are usually stages of meetings: first, an introductory session followed by paperwork; then intermediate gatherings as individuals are "worked up" in the ongoing process of evaluation and placement. Often, the prospective adoptive parents move up to a short list of expectant parents. It is increasingly common for agencies to show birth mothers (and birth fathers) profiles of these short-listed prospective parents and allow the birth parent to choose a family for the baby. More often, the birth mother is alone in the choosing. Sometimes, she requests a meeting with the family she has chosen; sometimes requests are made (for example, a promise that the child will have educational opportunities). All of this can occur before the baby is born and before the placement. It is part of the arduous waiting process on the part of the adoptive family.

Expectant waiting always involves not only the potential for gift, but the potential for loss. A birth mother or birth father can change her or his mind before the baby is born, after the baby is born, and after the baby has been placed with a family. Birth grandparents can decide to raise the baby. With older children, as we shall see in the case of Martha in chapter 5, there can be a mismatch between parent and child. With special-needs children, it can be later determined that a chosen family was not an appropriate fit with the needs of the child. International adoptions can encounter governmental and political delays. Yes, adoption has its risks; more so, I believe, than biological pregnancy. For these reasons, unlike the biological parent who may decorate the baby's room, shop for baby items, and have baby showers before the baby is born, the prospective adoptive parent often waits until the adoption is complete to do these things. The risks in the process lead to caution.

Alicia Fox, who is both a biological and an adoptive mother, after enumerating the challenges she faced adopting a baby from Peru, expressed the sense of expectant waiting: "The labor pains for this adoption were almost worse, longer, than they were for my biological daughter. Adoption was another way of giving birth. I am a new mother. My adopted son was born not of my flesh but of my hopes and dreams. God has given my two children to me to raise. And that is a gift."

The harmonic note of gift rises above the clash of discordant notes, flat with failure, and sharp with sourness that can impact an adoption. Rising triumphantly above the cacophony comes harmony in the medley of songs familiar to the adoptive parent who has finally been given a child. The medley has but one refrain: Children are a gift from God.

A Father-To-Be: Sam Cesaretti

Sam Cesaretti's story of expectant waiting reveals the deep yearning of a man for a child, his persistence in trying to hold on to his adopted son, his tenacity through loving anticipation and expectant waiting.

As I mentioned earlier, Sam is a Presbyterian minister, who with his wife Peggy adopted a son from Peru. Sam and Peggy ended their infertility treatments before they contacted an agency about international adoption. The following account of their experience of "expectant waiting" is told from the viewpoint of Sam, a father-to-be. Sam and Peggy's longing, their passionate search for a way to finalize the adoption, and their ecstatic reception of a child, their son, illustrate the idea of being embraced even as one is being relinquished.

Sam and Peggy arrived in Peru at seven in the morning. At nine, they held a tiny baby in their hands. He was three months old and pale, and Sam remembers that something "just didn't seem right." They learned that the baby had been hospitalized for ten days with dysentery because the foster mother had not cleaned the bottle nipples properly. When the birth mother found out the child was not well, she contacted the lawyer and made sure the baby received medical attention. He still bears scars from the IVs. The birth mother and the foster mother alternated days and nights in the hospital.

When Sam and Peggy arrived in Peru, their expectant waiting was extended by problem after problem. The fear and stress was manageable: They had each other, and they had tremendous support from Sam's church in the U.S. and from Sam's parents. Sam's church gave him a ten-week parental leave. "They just said, 'come back with the baby.' . . . I've never experienced anything in the church like that before—to receive that kind of grace and love." Cards, letters, phone calls, diapers—all came as a reminder of the support at home.

For adoptive parents, even after the baby is in their arms, the expectant waiting can continue for legal reasons. In Peru, even though Sam and Peggy had their baby, the expectant waiting continued because the documents were not signed. "In those ten weeks we hardly let Adam out of our sight. At least one of us was with him the whole time. That's what he needed. He had been in a hospital bed for ten days at the age of two months, on the verge of death, and he just needed to be held, and that's what we did. And that's what I largely did at night. It was just a frustrating experience, and more costly than we thought it would be. I knew something of the culture and knew that it would involve under-the-table payments, but they had us hostage. The adoption was done through an agency, which made the initial contact, but when we were down there . . . we were pretty much on our own."

The social worker in Peru misplaced the legal papers and was generally ineffective. Sam and Peggy feared they would have to return to the U.S. without the baby. Sam's mother contacted various government agencies and talked to their congressman. Sam needed the papers by noon one Friday or the adoption would have been extended by two months with Sam and Peggy waiting in Peru. "I still remember, at a quarter to twelve, Federal Express pulling up in front of our little hostel and depositing all those papers in our midst. It was just phenomenal. They pulled us through."

Peruvian politics also slowed the adoption. The judges went on strike for a while, and then the district attorneys. During the ten weeks, Sam and Peggy took gifts like computers, calculators, and perfume to various officials and others involved in the adoption. "One thing that kept us going," Sam explained later, "was first of all having a little baby there from the start . . . that was our reason and all. And even though he was sick, he just provided incredible joy even in the midst of all that." Sam's and Peggy's two families—

their parents and siblings together with their church family—shared in both the chaos and the elation of the expectant waiting.

In the course of their expectant waiting, Sam and Adam began to bond. This physical and emotional bonding is fairly common in biological pregnancy, particularly as the birth mother feels the baby move inside her and as the pregnancy develops. Sam likened his awareness of attachment to his faith experience: There was not one point in his life when he knew he was a Christian. Instead, there were certain points in both his faith experience and in his bonding with baby Adam that he knew something was going on.

"One moment took place at three o'clock at night. I was holding him; we were in the living room. Peggy was still sleeping. There was a light coming in from the lights outside, and the light came across his face, and his eyes met my eyes, and they just didn't move for five minutes. We just stared at each other. Instead of him just looking around, he just fixed on my eyes, and my eyes fixed on him. Once again, just like in my faith story, I can point to particular people who had an effect. I can think of particular moments like that. I can look back and say, 'you know, there's something going on here that's bigger than me, and bigger than both of us together. And that continues to happen."

Sam had been told by other adoptive parents that this might be the most difficult experience of his life. As he encountered delay after delay in Peru, he and Peggy persevered by concentrating on the future, on their purpose for being there, and on the child.

On the final day of their extended and complicated expectant wait in Peru, Sam went to get the exit visa that would allow them to leave with Adam. He had made reservations for one of the few flights to Miami, due to leave on a Thursday. Since the embassy was closed on Wednesdays, he had to get the exit visa on Tuesday. Failure to do so would mean an additional wait of two and a half weeks. Sam's lawyer instructed him to go to the main square in Lima and meet an unknown "coordinator." After a long wait, someone called his name. Another wait ensued. Sam needed to return to the embassy before eleven. From eleven to one the embassy closed and processed papers. Papers were then handed out at four; Sam needed Adam's birth certificate from the coordinator on the square in order to obtain the visa.

"We were standing underneath the big clock. It was 9:00—9:30—9:45—10:00—11:00—11:15. My heart was just sinking. We were supposed to be there by eleven." Sam waited for two hours before he realized the "coordinator" was expecting more money. Sam finally got the birth certificate at 12:15. He knew the embassy was closed. The birth certificate had to be translated into English, and Sam was next taken to a man who typed the translation in his car on a portable typewriter. By then, it was 12:30. Sam made it to the embassy—the closed embassy. His heart sank at the sight.

He recalled the story in the New Testament of a persistent woman going before a judge. He became that woman. "There were Peruvian guards out there with their weapons, and I said, 'I have to get in there' in my broken Spanish. They said, 'No, it's closed.' I said, 'You don't understand. I have to get there.' 'No, no. It's not possible.' For about ten minutes, I just stood there. I wouldn't give up. Finally one of the guys went down to the back of the building. He said he would go in and check. 'Nobody's there. You have to go home.' 'No, I have to get in there. You don't understand.' We argued some more and then finally he went back, and I went with him in a back door, and sure enough made it to the little window where we were supposed to hand these in three hours earlier. The blinds were drawn at the visa window.

I just started knocking on the window. Knocking. Knocking. Knocking. Finally a woman pulled the blind up and saw me and smiled. I gave the translation to her, and she took it and said, 'Okay, everything's okay.' And I went back to Peggy because Peggy was expecting me back by ten or so, and it was now 1:30 in the afternoon. This was the one time in the whole process where I just broke down and cried."

At four, Sam returned for the visa. Thirty people were waiting for visas, and he was not certain that his had really been processed. As one person after another received visas, the room eventually became empty. At the very last moment, he heard, "Mr. Cesaretti!"

A Mother-To-Be: Jane Rhodes

Every adoptive parent has a unique story of how the waiting period unfolded. Unlike some "expectant" mothers who prepare the baby's room, shop for clothes, and notify a wider range of friends of the adoption, Jane Rhodes handled the preparations more privately. Her lawyer advised that there was a risk of the adoption falling through, and Jane and her husband felt the need for self-protection.

Jane: "We had just returned from a meeting of Resolve, a national support group for infertile couples. That night, the symposium was on methods of adoption. It was about ten o'clock, and the phone rang; a physician said, 'There's good news. There is a baby.' My husband and I were stunned. We had only just learned that many couples were advertising and sending out résumés. We had been told to broaden our networks, to let more people like pastors, lawyers, doctors, friends know we wanted to adopt. I remember thinking, 'It's going to be a lot more work to send out those résumés,' when the phone rang.

"As it turned out, an old friend had been watching out for us in his private practice; an eleventh-grader had come to him, seven months pregnant. He recommended us. The lawyer he referred us to also knew us. And even though the birth mother lived in another state, the delivering obstetrician had been my brother's best friend in high school! We were so grateful that we had reached out for help two years earlier in contacting this physician and revealing our infertile situation.

"After the phone call, we wandered around the house in a daze. The next morning, I drove to work thinking, I'm going to be a mother. I'm going to be a mother. I began the expectant waiting: I signed up for a baby care course at a local hospital, I made a retreat to prepare myself inwardly for the baby's coming, I wrote a letter of joyfulness to the baby and a letter of total gratitude to the birth mother. We contacted a photographer to be on hand when we took the baby home from the hospital.

"We were afraid to convert a room into a nursery, because our lawyer informed us that the birth grandmother was reconsidering and was contemplating keeping the child. The birth mother was an only daughter, and her mother felt that this might be her only grandchild. At one point, the lawyer even told us the adoption was going to fall through. We had a lawyer in the state of the birth and a lawyer in our state; we quickly put them in touch with each other so that they could work together as a team.

"The birth mother wanted a place to live for a few weeks in the summer so that her high school friends would not know. Because this was a closed adoption, there was never a question of her living with us. I called several Christian friends in the city in which the baby was to be born. One older Christian woman found a private, Episcopalian home for the birth mother.

"We did not purchase any clothes or even tell friends. We lived with the possibility of the birth grandmother keeping the baby.

"I imagined that the baby was a girl. Our lawyer called us when the birth mother was in her eighth month to tell us the result of a sonogram. 'Do you know what the baby is?' he asked. 'A girl, I guess,' I replied. 'No, it's a boy!' Once again, we were stunned. My husband, with a dazed look, said, 'A boy. Oh my, I'm going to be a father. A boy. Oh my. Baseball, football, soccer.' Our theme song became 'Take Me Out to the Ballgame'. When we brought our son home from the hospital, my mother had a child's baseball cap and bat leaning against the crib.

"Our waiting didn't end then, however. We faced a waiting period of eleven more days in which, by state law, the birth mother could change her mind. I would do over again what we did, but this kind of waiting is stressful. The expectant waiting continues because the baby is not yours yet. My friends did not have any showers for me although they all stopped by with presents. I was in an awkward position. Here was this newborn for whom we had nothing; yet, the legal waiting period was not over. We were afraid to celebrate.

"On the night of the fourteenth day, the last day in which the birth mother could change her mind, at 14 minutes until midnight, the phone rang. My mother answered it. No one was there. At 13 minutes to midnight, the phone rang again. My father answered it. No one. At midnight, I climbed the stairs to the bedroom I shared with the baby, collapsed in the bed, and went into a deep sleep. The next day, friends called and said, 'You made it. We were praying for you.'

"After the private adoption of our son, we went through two failed agency adoptions, but I continued to wait. I wrote a letter to my future daughter and told her I wouldn't give up looking for her.

"When the agency called eight months after the more painful of the two failed adoptions, I was guarding my heart. We did not prepare anything, afraid of being hurt again. We were afraid to tell our son in case this was to be a third failed adoption. I wanted both children to have the same celebratory homecoming with relatives and photos and videos, but we told very few people. I did tell my best friend what was happening, and she stood by to rush out and buy an outfit at the last minute.

"In our state, the legal waiting period was ten days. The agency suggested that the birth mother let them place the baby girl in a foster home until the ten days were over, but she did not want the baby to go through too many changes. She kept the baby through the waiting period, took pictures, made a scrapbook, slept with her daughter. This was an open adoption, and I grew to admire and be quite fond of our daughter's birth mother, with whom we have stayed in touch through the agency. I have actually sent more pictures and notes than were asked of me because I know how much this birth mother loved her baby. When my daughter wants to meet her someday, I stand ready to facilitate that in every way. I want her to know she was doubly loved, maternally speaking."

Miscarried Adoption

Expectant adoptive parents also live with the possibility of loss. They are aware of the rates of miscarriage, delivery complications, and infant mortality that biological parents fear. A prospective adoptive parent may live with not only the grief following the inability to have a biological child but with the potential for loss of the hoped-for adopted child. A miscarried adoption is the most difficult of all adoption experiences.

According to the most recent analysis of adoption statistics, at least half of pregnant birth mothers who plan to part with their babies through adoption change their minds.[3] International adoptions are subject to changing regulations. I have known couples and singles to experience as many as three failed adoptions. It is wise to take a break from the adoption process in such a situation, just as a person would want to take a pause from prolonged, intensive infertility treatments.

Much has been written about the grieving of birth mothers and adoptees. One of my goals in this book is to document aspects of the grieving of adoptive parents. I believe that in the context of prior gynecological grief, a person celebrates uniquely when a baby is given to her/him. For example, if a person has known hunger or unemployment or fear, the gifts of food or work or safety will be appreciated against the backdrop of their former absence. The presence of these essentials are valued because of the memory of when they were not. Adoptive parents are acutely aware that a child is a gift from God, although in failed adoption, it is harder to make this affirmation.

Jane: "For years, I repeated the Apostles' Creed and never thought much about the phrase 'And he descended into hell.' If you experience a failed adoption, you descend into hell. You will be in a place of hopelessness and despair. You will be in the womb of Sheol.

"When I experienced a disrupted adoption, my first reaction was bitterness. We had been through too many surprises in the process. First, what was going to be a private adoption turned into an open adoption. Then, the birth mother interviewed us and set conditions. What we thought was one child turned out to be twins. After learning that one had a congenital heart defect, we again adjusted our expectations and our medical coverage . . . only to learn that the birth mother had changed her mind, cut off contact with us and the agency.

"Our vulnerability before, during, and after the births set me up for major grief. When a nurse first told me that our permission to receive medical updates and our visitation privileges had been rescinded, I was incredulous. The adoption counselor was not available until the situation was too complicated to resolve. That night I descended into hell. It was some comfort to know that Jesus had also been there. I knew that Jesus had also ascended. I was more focused on the descent.

"When the anger came, I could not direct it at the birth mother, for she had cut off contact abruptly. I could not direct it at the agency; my husband kept reminding me that we were still at the top of their list, after five years of wait-ing. 'Please don't jeopardize us!' he admonished. So the anger turned inward and into depression.

"That is when I called two friends who had also made the descent into hell. Their descents had been precipitated by abusive marriages and divorce. They had known great pain—and had survived. Both women stopped every-thing and lovingly, gently, carefully thrust a hand of humanity into the pit of Sheol [Ps. 16:10]. Both knew not to say, God is with you in the pain. I knew God was with me in the pain. It was that I didn't want to be in the pain anymore.

"One of the women, who knew the losses my husband and I had experi-enced in the previous six months, used the image of a person wounded on the battlefield. 'You have fought so many battles this year, you have so many wounds, don't try to crawl over and bandage someone else. Let the First Aid van come. And I'm one of the people on the First Aid truck!' She helped me to think of ways to receive aid. She knew that when the pain is that great, a person can want to die on the field. 'Let us bandage the wounds. Let people care for you.' I let the stretcher come.

"The image I focused on was a recovery room. After infertility surgery, the pain is so great, you don't care how many eggs were retrieved. You try to sit up, get nauseated, hear that your blood pressure has dropped, and collapse back on the stretcher. All you can think of is getting that first piece of ice. Then, the second. In the ascent from hell, you concentrate on lessening the pain. Being thankful for your blessings doesn't work. Nor do platitudes.

"What advice can I give? Stay with nurturing people. Stay in nurturing environments. Keep a suicide hotline number in your wallet. Keep your coun-selor's number close by, along with phone numbers of friends. Ask those few reliable friends who have also made the descent into hell if they will stand by at any hour of night. Take one day at a time. Read the Psalms. Remember that Christ descended into hell and is victor even over that. Do not concentrate on the plaque that says, 'Children are a gift from God.' Rather, focus on, 'Jesus Christ is Lord.'

" 'On the third day, he rose again from the dead, and ascended into heaven, where he sitteth on the right hand of God.'

"Those human hands are essential, too, when you descend into hell."

Events and feelings like those of Alicia Fox, Sam Cesaretti, and Jane Rhodes are all part of the *anxious waiting*, a time when you are sorely afraid the child might be taken away. It would not be fair to hold this back from prospective adoptive couples or singles. You have to want a baby very much and be willing to take some risks to go through what we did. You need a strong support group more than you need a nursery.

I hope these stories of waiting are told to the children so they will know how very much they were loved and wanted. I also hope that birth mothers know how much we value and respect them as mothers.

Expectant waiting, like adoption itself, contains the dual and dynamic elements of grief and gift. In a way, this reflects characteristics of God, as God experiences the grief over those lost to the family of faith as well as the joy of the coming of adopted sons and daughters. This dual dynamic mirrors the miscarried adoptions of some but also illustrates others coming home to God.

"A Little Well Filling Up"

The lounge of the Lutheran seminary was crowded with friends and fellow students. Kate had just returned from her trip to southern China, a journey that was a grand finale to many years of "expectant waiting" on the part of Liz, Kate's sister-in-law.

Liz had adopted a baby girl on the trip. Kate described Liz in tender words:

"Liz is a single professional woman who has been a loving, attentive aunt to our children throughout their lives. From the time she was a little girl, Liz knew she wanted a baby of her own. After the disappointment of a broken engagement, she began to come to terms with the reality that she might not ever give birth to a child or make her family in the 'traditional' way. She began the adoption process and, fourteen months later, received a picture of her new daughter."

With anticipation, Kate and Liz travelled to China with sixteen other families awaiting a baby and with two agency social workers. After two days in Beijing, Liz and Kate flew to southern China for the placement.

What impressed me about their experience was the expectancy of waiting in the hotel room as babies were delivered to eager parents. But the sensitivity on Liz's part with the delivery of the baby was quite evident in the video that Kate taped. Kate described this anticipative experience:

"We heard a knock at the door, and the social worker told Liz they would be bringing her baby next. I stepped into the hall to film the arrival. I tried to hold the camera steady as they rounded the corner—the social worker, translator, and caregiver, who held the baby. My breath caught at the beauty of this child. She had huge, dark, sensitive eyes and a shock of silky hair."

Now, one might expect idyllic moments from this point. On the contrary, the video documented the distraught crying, the inconsolable wailing, and the baby's desperate clinging to the caregiver's neck. And then, to me, the remarkable part of the delivery occurred. Liz, who had waited all these years to cradle a baby in her arms, just calmly sat down on the bed beside the baby who was still in the arms of the Asian caregiver. Liz learned about the baby's formula; she inquired where the baby had been found; she asked the caregiver to record a written message to the baby in a book. Liz gave the caregiver a bracelet and kept an identical one for her daughter. She learned how the baby liked to be comforted, what toys she preferred, who her crib-mate had been. Liz was concerned about a scar on the back of the baby's head and some erratic movements of the head and hands, all of which were explained as common behaviors for children who have been institutionalized. The social worker asked Liz how she felt about these things. "I couldn't leave her here," Liz replied unhesitatingly. At that moment Kate knew Liz's child was "home."

Throughout the somewhat chaotic delivery, Liz sat next to the baby, softly rubbing her stomach and legs and jiggling her feet. The music "Kum Ba Yah" played softly as a "comforting quiet fell over the room." The baby gradually got used to Liz's touch. In the ensuing days, as the adoptive families toured China and absorbed all they could of their children's country of birth, Liz carried her baby in a pouch. Kate passed on an image:

"Where she [the baby] had once resisted our attention, she now hugged us tightly around our necks. It was as though she couldn't get close enough. 'It's like a little well filling up,' the social worker said."

I had always thought of "expectant waiting" from the vantage point of the adoptive parents. Yet, here—on video—was a child from an institution in which she had spent hours alone in a crib, rubbing the back of her head against her crib so often that a scar formed, inventing games with her own hands for stimulation—here was a child who had also been expectantly waiting, for someone to be with her, to rub her, to play with her, to carry her in a pouch. She had been waiting to come home.

Adoption: It's like a little well filling up after weeks, months, years of expectant waiting.

Chapter 5

Homecoming

> *But, beneath or beyond all that, "coming home" meant, for me, walk-*
> *ing step by step toward the One who awaits me with open arms and*
> *wants to hold me in an eternal embrace. I knew that Rembrandt*
> *deeply understood this spiritual homecoming. I knew that, when Rem-*
> *brandt painted his Prodigal Son, he had lived a life that left him with*
> *no doubt about his true and final home.*
> (*Henri J.M. Nouwen, The Return of the Prodigal Son*)

*T*he homecoming of a long-expected child is a homecoming into the welcoming heart. This is true for both biological and adopted children. For biological children, there is usually a departure from the hospital after a nurse or
aide has helped the new mother to the car. Sometimes grandparents or other
family members make up an entourage. If flowers or balloons have been sent
to the hospital or birthing suites, these usually accompany the new parent(s)
home. Neighbors or relatives may have food prepared and the house cleaned
to welcome the new mother and baby. With a home birth, the homecoming
might be the birth of the child in familiar surroundings.

A homecoming for an adopted child is the placement or the entrance of a
child into the life of a family or an individual. Usually, there is jubilation, gai-
ety, celebration amidst ceremony, gifts, parties, an influx of relatives and
friends, a reception at the airport. Homecoming can, of course, also be surrounded by diapers, diarrhea, and disabilities. But it always involves a unique
bondedness between parent and child. The one constant is the hospitable
heart.

William Fisch spoke of these instincts of attachment following the adoption of his infant son, Nick. When their son began cutting teeth at four months
of age, he cried often during the night and needed comforting. During one
long week of sleep deprivation, Fisch offered to make the trips down to the

first floor nursery alone in order that his wife could sleep uninterrupted. On one of those nights, after rocking his son for five hours and trying to put him back into his crib, father and son dozed off in the rocker. Upon waking at dawn, Fisch gazed at his son snuggled in his arms and wrote of his attachment:

"Almost immediately I could feel the warmest, deepest feelings well up inside of me from way down in my soul. I felt the most powerful feelings of belonging and attachment toward this little boy. Instantly, I felt the same feelings inside of me that I learned to feel for my dad, and 'from' my dad, many years ago. This bonding feeling brought forward memories of my dad."[1]

Fisch described his vivid memories, especially the night his father went looking for him, lost in a fog, and he wrote:

"The fog incident brings to my mind the thought of a man who loves his boys enough to get out of bed on a foggy night and go out and search the highways and roads, not knowing what he may find. I will always remember the long lonely night in that bedroom when the loving bond for my son began to truly develop into the same loving bond that I had with my own father."[2]

The hospitable heart may well be one that has absorbed past disappointments. The most striking example in Scripture of this type of welcome in homecoming is found in the story of the Prodigal Son, who, after many profligate experiences, returns to an overjoyed father. A party is thrown, as the mood of celebration is foremost.

> So he [the son] set off and went to his father. But while he was still far off, his father saw him and was filled with compassion; he ran and put his arms around him and kissed him. . . . The father said to his slaves, "Quickly, bring out a robe—the best one—and put it on him; put a ring on his finger and sandals on his feet. And get the fatted calf and kill it, and let us eat and celebrate; for this son of mine was dead and is alive again; he was lost and is found!" And they began to celebrate. (Luke 15:20, 22–24)

A contemporary version of joyful homecoming is told by Ed Loring, cofounder of Atlanta's Open Door Community, a ministry and place of hospitality. In a sermon, Loring creates a present-day Prodigal Daughter. A mama's younger child, a daughter, leaves home to waste herself in reckless, wild living. She uses crack cocaine, has multiple sex partners, and lives in poverty. But then she comes to her senses: "I will get up and go to my mother and say, 'Mama, I have turned away from God and disrespected you. . . . I am no longer fit to be called your daughter; treat me as one of your part-time employees.'" So she starts back home.

"She was still several blocks from home when her mother saw her baby get off the Marta bus; her mama's heart was filled with compassion, and she ran, threw her arms round her daughter, and hugged and kissed her. The daughter confesses. Pierced to the center of her heart, but acting as though she heard not a word, the mother called her employees. They are to find the best clothes, wash her feet, bring the favorite foods, and celebrate the homecoming."[3]

The biblical story of the Prodigal Son and its contemporary rendition, the Prodigal Daughter, offer an image of a homecoming. The artist Rembrandt van Rijn painted at least two versions of the return of the Prodigal Son as described in Luke 15. The most beloved painting was acquired by Catherine the Great in 1766 and hangs in The Hermitage of Saint Petersburg, Russia. The late Henri Nouwen, author of *The Return of the Prodigal Son*,[4] felt that Rembrandt's painting of the father clasping the returning son to himself was a depiction of true homecoming. In this chapter I offer contemporary portraits of what homecoming is like for families created through adoption.

There are as many portraits or variations of homecoming as there are parents. The heart of the parent in the parable of the Prodigal is wide open, filled with compassion or womb-love. Homecoming is a cause for celebration. Both the father of the Prodigal Son and the mother of the Prodigal Daughter had known pain, much like Connie in the following story. None of the parabolic parents are certain that the future will be problem-free. Yet, their joy is so overwhelming at the moment of homecoming, even we as readers are caught—for a moment—in an eternal embrace.

Connie: "Our Souls Met"

Like the father and mother of the Prodigals, Connie Gauley had known disappointment. She had experienced a miscarriage. After going through therapy to work on her grief, she cared for two foster children. She and her husband, Ed, later took in a third foster child, Robbie, who was thirteen weeks old and a "failure-to-thrive baby." His birth mother had abandoned him at six weeks, and Robbie had been placed in a group foster home for seven weeks.

Connie says that he looked like a little frog and, sadly, asked for nothing. She took him to a department store to have his picture taken; she didn't want him to lack a baby photo in kindergarten when all the other children were bringing their baby pictures. "The first week of January, I had a clue that something was wrong, because he just didn't ask for anything. I had a collection of dinner bells . . . and I rang them, and he never responded." She thought he was deaf, but after medical tests, physical impairments were eliminated; his lack of response was simply the failure to thrive. Connie attributed some of this to his grieving the loss of his birth mother. The doctors also discovered that Robbie couldn't move his head to the left, probably because a bottle had been propped on his right side in the group home.

Connie started breaking the rules of "good foster parenting"; for example, she put him in her bed at night when he woke up crying, constantly tending to him physically and emotionally. The homecoming occurred toward the end of January, after she'd had him for several weeks. "He'd lay on the floor, and I'd lay over top of him, you know, on all fours. And I'd kiss his left cheek, then I'd kiss his right cheek, and I'd kiss his left cheek and I'd stop, you know, in between, and I'd kiss back and forth. . . . I kissed his left cheek, and he turned his head for me to kiss his right cheek, and I just started to cry! It was so wonderful because it was the first thing he'd ever asked anybody for. . . . He never asked to be fed, he never asked to be held, he never asked for anything, and that was the first thing he asked me for: to kiss the other side. . . . It was something we did every day, you know, just to kiss him back . . . from side to side. And he turned his cheek and asked to be kissed."

It was 1986, and in those days, social services did not allow foster parents to adopt the children in their care. But after Robbie's birth mother officially abandoned him, Connie and her husband hired a lawyer and successfully lobbied to adopt him. They had had other foster children before and had others after Robbie; Connie also became pregnant and birthed a child. Throughout all this, she held firm to the belief that Robbie was meant for their family. When doctors suspected he had cerebral palsy, she held steady. Through physical, speech, and occupational therapy, she never wavered.

"Our souls met," she maintained. "It was a perfect match. I could never thank him enough for what he gave me. He gave me what I always wanted to be. I always wanted to be a mom. And you know, until him, I didn't get to be that. How can you not love somebody who does that for you?"

The homecoming occurred when Robbie turned his cheek, searching and asking for affection. Like the Prodigal Son in the Scriptures, Robbie allowed himself to be kissed. According to Connie, this was homecoming, when their souls met.

Linda and Harry: "A Honeymoon with a Child"

Linda and Harry Turnbull are busy lawyers. The adoption process afforded them unpressured time to enjoy their baby son, Richard. After receiving their son in Peru, they spent a leisurely six weeks in Lima waiting for the adoption to be finalized. At first, Harry and Linda marked July 28, Peruvian Independence Day and the date of the flight back to the U.S. with their son, as the day of "homecoming." The airline had put them up in a hotel on the main square of Lima due to a plane delay. Linda and the baby watched as Peruvians celebrated Independence Day below their window.

On reconsideration, however, Harry and Linda both decided their homecoming was really their time in Peru. For six weeks, they had "a honeymoon with a child" and were all by themselves. There were no interruptions, no phones, no demands from clients, no relatives. There are "so few times to get a six-week break," admits Harry. Linda saw the time as a vacation as she nestled Richard in a front pack and set out to discover Peru. They took tours of the country, sampled local cuisine, danced together to Peruvian music with their baby. They talked to people and got to know the country. Each described their "honeymoon with a child." Harry: "We got up in the morning and very leisurely went out to get pastries and a newspaper and sat around." Linda: "We spent a lot of time just being." To them, homecoming is a warm memory; it is the time they became a family of three.

Dena: "A Real Celebration Day"

Dena Hogan, a single woman, waited through years of infertility and three failed adoptions before she traveled to Peru to pick up her infant daughter, Leah, who had been born in a dirt hut to a twenty-six-year-old mother.

"In Peru, the night before I got Leah, I was in bed and I dreamed that I was pregnant. Someone said, 'Oh, you are pregnant,' and I said, 'Yes.' They said, 'Aren't you worried about the delivery process?' And I said, 'No, because I've already seen this baby and she's a beautiful little girl. Her name is Leah.'"

The next day, in an old VW taxi, accompanied by a translator, Dena drove into the slums to view the sickly baby, her baby, who lay curled in a fetal position. Two and a half months old, she weighed only eight pounds. Dena was told to come back the next day for her baby, but during the night, Dena became seriously ill with food poisoning. Fearing her child would be gone, she arrived a day late for the "homecoming," but the baby was waiting, and they left together celebrating. She showed her baby to the other waiting American families crowded in designated apartments in Peru. Dena called her parents and friends. "It was a real celebration day. She'd never been to the doctor, so I took her right away. She was filthy dirty, and I bathed her. I probably did the same thing everyone did—staying up all night, looking in the crib, making sure she was still breathing. I took a zillion pictures with video. It was wonderful. It was thrilling. Then we had eight more weeks of time to spend together. I can never say enough about that time." Dena had eight, uninterrupted weeks to carry her baby in a pouch, walk the streets and markets, sit in outdoor cafes and sip wine with her baby on her chest. She knew she was facing a return to the corporate world and relished the time in Peru as a luxury.

Her emotional bonding with her daughter was intense and instant. "I was really just attached to her right away. We were such buddies. Immediately. And I just thought she was the most wonderful little girl." Dena asked to meet her daughter's birth mother again and worked through a translator. She showed her a picture of what the baby's room would look like in America. "One whole room just for her?" queried the tiny Peruvian birth mother. Before Dena and the baby were to leave Peru, the birth mother asked to see the baby one more time and produced a letter. "She reached into the pocket of her apron and pulled out a letter. Impoverished, with no resources, living in the ghetto, she had nonetheless found someone to write a letter in English. . . . It said, 'I never realized I would find myself in such desperate circumstances, and I want you to know I love you.'"

When Dena returned home, about forty friends waited at the airport to celebrate the homecoming. But the homecoming for mother and child had already taken place in those slow days in Peru.

Dena had been raised with siblings and wanted a larger family. Less than two years later, she applied with the same agency for a second adoption. Within two months, she was back in Peru. Her parents cared for her daughter back in the States.

When she first saw her son, Peter, "He was just in the pink of health and very bright and active and a sweet baby boy." Anticipating that the adoption would drag on for months, as her earlier one had, and hesitant to leave her daughter for that long, she put him in a recommended foster home in Peru. This particular foster home was run by a friend of her adoption coordinator. The day she left Lima, the Iraqi war broke out, and a bombing occurred in the airport parking lot. Amidst mangled cars and machine guns, Dena feared for her life and her son's.

She called each week from the United States to check on her son, receiving positive reports of his health and development from the foster care workers. Although adoptions were generally taking a long time, four weeks after she left, Dena was notified that the adoption process was completed in Peru. She flew back to Lima and was met at midnight by a car; inside was Peter, wrapped in blankets.

"It wasn't until I got back inside my apartment and unwrapped his blankets that I realized that he had been seriously neglected. Thank goodness I was only gone four weeks. It was another act of God that I got down there when I did. Everybody else's papers for some reason took longer, but mine suddenly were done in four weeks. If it had taken longer, I am sure he wouldn't have lived. . . . When I left him, he was a fat, happy baby. I came back and he was squirting diarrhea, and he had open sores on the soles of his feet. He was covered with eczema and scabies and had some horrible parasite. . . . I was just in shock. Another waiting American looked at him and burst into tears. Other families waiting to adopt looked away."

On the airplane, she mixed a drink like Pedialyte, an oral electrolyte maintenance solution that doctors recommend for dehydration. "We got into Miami and I numbly walked through the airport and boarded a plane for home."

For six weeks, his health worsened. Dena didn't go back to work, putting her job on hold. Eventually, her son was hospitalized. Doctors ran many tests. The Center for Disease Control in Atlanta was contacted. Various diseases were ruled out. He spiked a high fever, and Dena's parents packed their bags once again and drove across country to help.

Finally, doctors identified a bacterial infection and began treatment. Dena's son began to respond. "He never would have made it in Peru," she believes. "And so it was a very different adoption experience for me than was adopting my daughter. With her, it was filled with joy from the beginning. And with him, it was very hard. And I think that I really didn't bond with him until after the medical crisis was through. Everybody thought he was going to die." This hesitancy to bond is not uncommon with parents who for medical or legal reasons fear such loss.

During the second homecoming, Dena's friends and her parents helped care for her daughter. Her employer kept her job intact. In the somber homecoming of a gravely ill infant, she found the faithful outstretched arms of those who loved her and her ailing son.

This is not so far removed from a scene in which a distinguished father saw a dirty, emaciated son coming from a far country and was filled with compassion. "He ran and put his arms around him and kissed him" (Luke 15:20b). This is homecoming, too.

Martha: "We Were Not Set to Do This"

Martha Brimmer, a physician in Madison, Wisconsin, tells of a child who came home, but did not stay. Years after this thwarted homecoming, her concern, love, and especially her pain are still there. This may be a form of miscarried adoption. Again, a miscarried adoption is the womb bereft of a desired-for child, the arms devoid of that maternal embrace. A failed homecoming mirrors the anguish that is also part of God's compassion and mercy or *rahum*, God's womb-love.

A month after her adoption miscarried, Martha entered a specialty of medicine that deals with troubled children and teens. She daily sees families in great pain.

"The death of my father and that miscarried adoption have been the hardest things I have ever had to deal with," she says. "Failed adoption is very hard. Ours is not a story with a happy ending. . . . We had two biological children quickly together. We had a perfect family situation; we moved to Madison. I wanted to have a larger family; we had the resources. My only concern is whether the young man we brought to this country was harmed by this whole experience. That I will probably never know. He should be 18 or 19 now."

Martha felt that families who did not have biological children should have newborns; she was willing to take an older child, around six years of age. She contacted a prominent international agency. The paperwork was complicated, and the process involved rigorous interviews.

Martha and her husband waited for four years with their agency. During this waiting period, workshops on adoptive parenting were offered by the agency, although Martha does not remember any focus on difficulties surrounding adoption. There was no mention that older adoptees often come from a background of abuse and neglect. The child later placed with Martha and Carl had been given up at age four by a man not his father. They had no information of what those four years entailed. Nor were they warned that it is more difficult to adopt an older child who has ties to his/her homeland.

Pictures went back and forth between Madison and the orphanage. A photo of their prospective son was in their home for two years while the process continued. Martha began bonding through the photos. She and Carl took several months off from work to help complete the process, eventually travelling to Bangkok. In Bangkok, they were taken from their hotel to the orphanage. There were eighty metal cribs covered with mosquito netting. Martha and Carl's child was now eight years old and still in a crib. All the children were sprinkled with baby powder to keep the insects off. "The people were gentle and nice. It was not a Dickensian scene. It was not negative," Martha recalls. But from her first view of the child's thin body, she knew she could not love him as she did her own biological children. "I had a negative physical reaction," she acknowledges. "I felt terrible. I felt like I had made the biggest mistake in my life. That was before he ever opened his mouth or before we had the problems with his behaviors. It was a physical, gut reaction. I was sick to my stomach and didn't know what to do with that. I felt incredible guilt."

She and her husband took their child to the hotel. After a couple of days, he started to cut himself and then tried to commit suicide by jumping out of the hotel windows. "He would tantrum hours on end, screaming at the top of his lungs. We were helpless in the hotel." Martha began to realize the impact of taking this child out of a culture and surroundings that were familiar to him, from a culture that disdained non-familial adoption. Fortunately, in the decade that has ensued since Martha's experience, clinicians and adoption researchers have been able to document this volatile reaction of international adoptees toward losing their familiar culture to these "strangers," i.e., adoptive parents. Hopefully, with heightened psychological understanding of what triggers an older child's violent reaction to well-intentioned adopting parents, the asymmetry between the child's view of the new parents as interlopers and the adults' view of themselves as parents will be anticipated, acknowledged, and absorbed.[5]

However, for Martha and Carl, there was no help in understanding their son's destructive behavior. The Thai and American social workers encouraged them to take him to America anyway, and said they would find another family once he was in America. Carl and Martha consented, despite their serious concerns. He screamed on the airplane ride to the United States. The social workers who accompanied the flight would ask him, "Don't you want a family? Don't you want a family?" Confused, he would answer "yes." He had had the picture of Martha's family over his bed for two years, just as they had had his. He called Martha and her husband "mom and dad" right away, but his frantic behaviors continued and were difficult for Martha's family. For example, shortly after their return to Madison, he ransacked the room of their biological son. His tantrums continued. "I realized I was bringing someone into my family I was not prepared to deal with. . . . My marriage was suffering. We had been together seventeen years. I became depressed." Martha went on antidepressants to function. She was not sleeping. Her husband withdrew from her and the family. Social workers recognized both the demise of the adoption and the maelstrom erupting in the family. In a matter of weeks, they were able to locate another family who had adopted a child from Thailand five years earlier and who had support from Thai-speaking professionals. Martha and her husband had not completed the legal adoption process and eventually handed the boy over to the social workers. "I can replay that sense of incredible depression and guilt that I felt. . . . I drive by the [location where the boy was relinquished to social workers]; it is a constant reminder of leaving that child."

Martha's story is of a misguided adoption. It challenges the theological image in the parable of the Prodigal Son, the image of a joyous parent welcoming home a wandering child. Where do Martha and Carl Brimmer fit in this parable? They meant to be the welcoming parents of a son coming from a distant country to their open home. Their motive was surely reflective of the father in the parable. Their position of welcome is reflective of but not identical to the parent in the parable, for the father in the parable is God to whom the child from Bangkok may always come. We can pray for that embrace of God, wide enough in compassion for all those caught in a misguided adoption.

Denise: "We All Had Fallen in Love"

Homecoming can be unpremeditated. It can occur without planning. This was the case with Denise and her husband, who were visiting professors in Indonesia. The family was from Holland, and both parents were connected to a theological seminary.

Denise and some of the students made clothes, and every Monday took them to a neighboring orphanage. These Monday afternoon visits were planned. The orphanage was always very clean on Mondays. But one day, not a Monday, Denise made an unannounced visit to the orphanage, and her life changed.

"The sight was terrible. It was so dirty. There were twenty-five babies in one room, and they didn't have diapers on. They just had to lay there on a kind of plastic oil cloth. It was a terrible mess. I said to the nurse there, 'What about this one?' And she said, 'well, that one will die this week.' She said it very, very 'matter of factly,' so I just acted without thinking." Denise was allowed to take the baby home to her husband and four sons. The baby, a girl, was very ill. Denise cleaned her and took her to a doctor. The child was diagnosed with double pneumonia; she was only four months old, very skinny and small. The baby recovered in a few weeks and turned into a lively infant with a smile. Denise remarks, "We all had fallen in love with her, so we thought, we will not bring her back to the orphanage."

The baby whom they named Esther lived with them a year before they returned to Holland. They hired a Dutch lawyer who facilitated the official adoption. Denise learned the baby's history. Her mother had died in a tiny Indonesian village while giving birth to this baby girl, her tenth child. Common folklore attributed the death of the mother to the child, and she became an outcast, considered to have an evil power. Her brothers and sisters transported her to the orphanage, half a day's walking distance from their village.

Back in Holland, Esther learned in kindergarten that babies came from their mothers' tummies. Denise was honest with her four-and-a-half-year-old: "You came from the tummy of your first mother, but I'm your second mother, and we found you, and I took you home, for you were very ill." At bedtime many nights as she grew older, Esther asked for the story about her "first mother" and ended the recounting with, "Well, it doesn't matter, because I have you."

Regarding the homecoming of her unexpected daughter, Denise confesses, "Adoption had never come into our minds. I had never thought about it. When I took her, it was not with the thought of adopting her. I took her in response to the nurse's words, 'Well, that one will die this week.'"

The one constant in these varying accounts is the hospitable heart. This can welcome the long-hoped-for child as in Connie's, Dena's, and Linda's and Harry's cases, or the unanticipated child in Denise's account. Homecoming can take place in a foreign country, in an airport, or at a parent's home address. It may differ in terms of geographical location, but never in the regions of the heart. We cannot forget Martha's welcoming heart, although her child did not come home to stay with her. The welcoming heart may absorb both past loss and the possibility of future woundedness. The homecoming of an adopted child can place us close spiritually to an eternal embrace of God, our true and final home.

Chapter 6

Growing Pains

On her child Jessy's autism:

> *Through this we have learned the lesson that no one studies willingly, the hard, slow lesson of Sophocles and Shakespeare—that one grows by suffering. And that too is Jessy's gift. I write now what fifteen years past I would still not have thought possible to write: that if today I were given the choice, to accept the experience, with everything that it entails, or to refuse the bitter largesse, I would have to stretch out my hands—because out of it has come, for all of us, an unimagined life. And I will not change the last word of the story. It is still love.*
> *Clara Claiborne Park, The Siege*

Adolescence is complicated for everyone, but can be especially challenging for adopted children.[1] They may face additional difficulties because of their personal histories, which may include prenatal neglect causing physical problems later, prenatal substance abuse by the birth mother, abuse prior to adoption, frequent changes of caregivers before adoption, and because of such issues as genealogical information gaps, differing parent-child temperaments and abilities ("mismatching" between adoptive parents and adoptee), and the child's intense struggle with personal identity. Certain "growing pains" may be more severe or more complex for an adopted child than a biological child. The National Adoption Information Clearinghouse (NAIC) offers additional psychological material about the impact of adoption on the stages of development.[2]

In this chapter, I focus on three types of growing pains that adopted adolescents encounter: identity confusion around the reality of their two sets of parents, grief about being relinquished by their birth parents, and an intensified awareness of the implications of this relinquishment. In a child's developing years, it is essential for a parent to have spiritual resources from which to draw. Some of the spiritual resources that adoptive families have used in the difficult phases of pre-adolescence and adolescence are offered at the conclusion of this chapter through the interviews with Nan and Steve Brown, Jeff Sawyer, and Jacob.

There is some disagreement among professionals on this issue of the development of adolescent adoptees. Sociologist David Kirk, for example, has questioned whether adoptive parents as well as specialists in adoption make too much out of the adopted child's difficulties, identifying signals and image problems that do not exist. "But," he recognizes, "we must also recall that where the cultural script is inadequate, the tune has to be played by ear; the artists have to improvise and that implies taking risks. Our question has to be whether the best calculated risk is in the direction of too little or too much sensitivity to the child's activities."[3] Despite his honest questions, Kirk suggests that parents should err on the side of too much sensitivity.

Kirk also counsels parents to assume authority. In his opinion, adoptive parents sometimes also experience "role handicap," a reticence to assume authority in parenting their non-biological child. Some of this he attributes to "genealogical bewilderment," a deficit of information about a child's biological heritage and the perplexity in knowing how to handle a child who is so very different from one's self.

It is my observation that most adoptive parents are not waiting for this professional debate to be resolved. They are generally more conscientious, sensitive, and meticulous in their attention to their child's health, activities, and welfare than other parents in their peer groupings. Sometimes, they may be overconscientious, oversensitive, overmeticulous. This arises, I believe, out of the hardwon realization that having a child is not a given. For the infertile, the myth that one day their bodies would produce a baby was shattered. Out of this disheveled myth, out of this climate of powerlessness, comes a keen appreciation of a child as gift and of the giving as grace. For those without an infertility history who are adopting out of religious, altruistic, or humanitarian reasons, the homecoming of a child into their family is often part of a calling or sense of vocation. The infertile and the fertile who adopt may travel different paths, but those paths converge at one terminal point of understanding: A child is not a given, but a gift.

Identity Development

The search for identity is difficult for all children today. For the adopted child, the quest to answer "Who am I?" is even more complicated. Adopted children are "twice born"[4]: first, by nature; second, by nurture. They are born by nature, from the union of the bodies of their birth parents, whose genetic traits will influence their development. They are born by nurture into the hearts and souls of the adoptive parents.

Adoptees' attitudes and responses to their adoptions vary, of course. A child may idealize the birth parents and thereby psychologically impact their own self-image. Some children, for example, may say things like, "My birth mother is a movie star and my real father is a great athlete." This kind of unrealistic comment is the result of a defense mechanism called "splitting" in which the child draws clear evaluative lines between the two sets of parents: good birth parents / bad adoptive parents. The mechanism of splitting people into good and bad can also work in reverse; the adoptee may identify herself as having bad birth parents / good adoptive parents. Splitting is most likely to occur in adolescence, when the adopted child may chafe at the normal parental restrictions, curfews, and limits set for the teenager.

Adopted children may also feel anger toward their birth parents, particularly their birth mothers, for relinquishing, for "unchoosing" to keep them. Or it may surface in response to adoptive parents' emphasis on "choosing" to keep her/him.

It is normal in the struggle to become an adult individual, in the process of identity formation, that the adolescent separates enough from her or his parents to establish a secure identity *vis-a-vis* (lit. face to face) the parents. Biological children, who share a genetic connectedness and often a physical resemblance with their parents, work at separating themselves from their parents in large part because they share a gene pool and, often, physical and temperamental similarities.

But from which set of parents do adopted adolescents separate and individuate, or form into a distinct personality? The birth parents or the adopted parents? Consider a situation in which the adopted child is very different in temperament, skin color, or abilities from the adopting parents: for example, an aggressive, extroverted child in a reserved family; an athletic, physical child in a shy, intellectual family; an African American child in a Caucasian family. While it is certainly true that a biological child can be very different from his or her biological parents in physical and behavioral characteristics, the percentage of marked differences between parent and child is higher with adopted children. These differences mean that even the process of identifying with one's parents in preparation to begin healthy separation and individuation is more complicated for the average adopted adolescent teenager.

Human beings develop in phases or stages, and each stage has a central issue that needs resolution. Erik Erikson, in *Identity: Youth and Crisis*, focused on psycho-social developmental stages that revolve around core crises.[5] Each of his "eight ages" has a core crisis containing a scale or spectrum of responses, ranging from a negative, or unfavorable, resolution to a positive, or favorable, resolution. Resolution of a core crisis ideally tends toward the positive pole of the spectrum. Focusing on the psycho-social "age of puberty and adolescence," Erikson identified the core crisis as identity versus role confusion. Ideally, the adolescent's struggle in this crisis would result in a resolution nearer to identity consolidation (the positive pole of the spectrum of responses) rather than role confusion (the negative pole). The healthy outcome of "identity consolidation" includes a basic sense of who one is in the world, as opposed to the absence of a clear sense of personal identity.

My research has shown that adopted children face more issues in their hunt for identity consolidation than Erikson imagined, for his psycho-social schema was developed with biological children/adolescents in mind. Building on Erikson's description of the successful outcome of the core crisis of identity formation as "identity consolidation," I have developed the term *identity dissolution* to identify a fragmentation of the disparate, or different, parts of the adopted child's identity.[6] The adopted child has two sets of parents, perhaps two sets of siblings, perhaps four sets of grandparents. These players will be, variously, major, minor, or even ghost players, but they are all there in the psyche of the adoptee. Identity development for the adoptee will generally take much more energy, time, love, and insight than it will for the non-adopted.

Erikson maintained that the core crisis of identity had to be positively resolved before true intimacy with another adult could take place. Some take issue with this sequence and argue that intimacy often precedes identity formation.[7] But no matter where professionals side in this debate, we can surely agree that identity formation affects intimate relationships. Before the psychological label of "attachment disorder" is so quickly applied by mental health professionals to an adolescent adoptee who is having difficulty with emotional bonding, we would be wise to consider the intricate relationship between identity formation and intimacy.

There is room for optimism, however, in the fact that domestic adoptions, by and large, are tending toward more openness, including openness to birth parents' continuing involvement in the adoption, accessibility to medical history records and birth certificates, candor regarding the details of the adoption, and encouragement of reunions between adoptees and birth parents. As adoptees know more about both sets of parents (birth and adopted), they will truly be able to know whose they are and who they are.

Faith resources will be needed by both adoptive parents and adoptees alike on the long and arduous journey of identity consolidation. It is best to let an adoptee help us understand how her faith entered into her identity search.

Mary Jo

Mary Jo was adopted as an infant by an infertile couple who were allowed to choose between several babies born in a home for unwed mothers. They chose her because she was actively looking around the room, instead of passively lying down. It was a closed adoption. Two years later, Mary Jo's parents adopted a son, Isaac. Nine years after this second adoption, Mary Jo's mother, at age thirty-eight, unexpectedly became pregnant and gave birth to Hope, a daughter. Mary Jo's parents made her feel as loved as her sister, affirming her with statements such as, "We didn't wait for you for nine months, we waited for you for three years," and "We actually went out and sought you."

When she was in fifth grade, around age eleven, Mary Jo began to ask, "Who am I?" She was reading the Scriptures and latched onto the verses about adoption in Eph. 1:5, Gal. 4:4–5, and Rom. 8:15. "That's it, that's who I am, I am an adopted child of God," she realized.

> "I knew what it meant. It meant two things. It meant that I was not exactly the same as God because an adopted child knows by instinct that they are not exactly the same as their parents. By the same token, all of those stories about my parents waiting for me and choosing me got [absorbed] into my understanding of the fact that God wanted me. It really did form my soul."

Mary Jo recalled a dream about Jesus that she had when she was very small. In it a voice said, "We wanted you and love you more and not less . . . we picked you out . . . you are our special child." Somehow her adoptive mother was on the edge of the dream. This dream and the loving words of her parents merged to give Mary Jo a positive sense of herself as adopted.

Mary Jo felt that it was easier for her to be an individual in her family because she was not related by DNA. Her first attempt at individuation, deciding on her own identity, was to begin playing a musical instrument in the sixth grade, something no one in her family would ever have done, and she has also made lifestyle and professional choices very different from those of her family.

She has a strong concept of God as perfect Adopting Parent, who not only serves as a model for earthly adopting parents, but can compensate when an adopted child encounters gaps in nurturing. To adoptive parents who feel they fall short as parents, Mary Jo offers this advice: "God's grace as an adoptive parent is big enough for you too."

Grief

Loss is a part of life. Until recently, however, there was no formal recognition of the role of grief in the adoption process. Rather, well-intentioned social workers and adoption facilitators implied that once an adoption was finalized, the family's life would be normal: that is, as normal as—and just like—life in a biologically related family.

More recently, however, research has identified the grief processes that everyone involved in adoption goes through, and we now know that it is a mistake to ignore or underestimate the interplay of grief, guilt, and gift (see chapter 1). We have previously looked at the joy of the homecoming, the reception of a child into a welcoming home. Now it is time to consider the multiple losses encountered in adoption.

For decades adoption was framed by parents and counseling professionals in terms of "chosenness." Adopted children were told they had been sought, singled out, and chosen by their adopting families. The landmark book parents used to explain this concept of chosenness to their children was *Chosen Baby* by Valentina P. Wasson.[8] Published in 1939, this book dominated the literature in children's adoption books until the 1990s.

More recently, some professionals have begun reevaluating the idea of chosenness and have identified other serious issues related to loss in adoption. Psychoanalytic clinician Paul Brinich has identified the various losses people suffer in adoption:

> The adoptive parents lose their view of themselves as fertile; they also lose the imaginary biological child conceived in their fantasies. The relinquishing parents lose a real child who is replaced by fantasies that cannot be corrected by exposure to the light of reality. These losses need to be recognized for what they are—neither less nor more—and they must be mourned.[9]

Brinich also identifies adopted children as "unwanted children," whose grieving must, in part, include coming to terms with the fact that their biological parents did not want them. "Usually," he argues, "a child is available for adoption only because he was *un*wanted."[10] Brinich's characterization flies in the face of what parents have historically told their adopted children.

An adopted child is normally made to feel very special because they have been chosen. At a certain cognitive developmental level, however, the adopted child realizes there is a reverse or flip side to chosenness: "unchosenness," or relinquishment. This awareness generally comes when a child is able to move intellectually from concrete to abstract concepts. In addition, the increasing numbers of open adoptions, coupled with research into the motivations of relinquishing birth parents done by sociologists such as Christine Swientek, have shown that children placed into the hands of adoptive parents are also almost always "wanted" by their birth mothers. The ambivalence that a birth mother generally feels is usually about her ability to care for her child in light of her social and economic circumstances.

I believe mental health researchers like Brinich not only overstate the "unchosen" aspect of adoption, they are mechanistic in viewing adoption as "an accident of personal history."[11] An accident of personal history implies a randomness, as in a throw of the dice; it relegates an occurrence to the realm of happenstance or, at best, fate. In making this claim, mental health researchers impart to the word "adoption" a negative nuance. Brinich's analysis of adoption is quite harsh: "It is impossible to understand adoption from an intrapsychic point of view without taking into account these two facts: first, that the child was not wanted by his biological parents; and second, that the adoptive parents were unable to conceive."[12]

For Christians, however, adoption is an affirmation of God working in life histories. Adoption is not an accident in a mechanical and impersonal universe; it is an action of God to meet the needs of all the members of the adoption triangle. God's agency is at work as most adoptive families sense a matching up of their children with their families. No matter what their children's growing pains, I have never met one adoptive parent who fails to see the triumph of gift in the process—the gift of a child.

In the course of normal psycho-social development, an adoptee may be focused on rejection or unchosenness at a particular stage. This commonly occurs in adolescence when identity and intimacy issues are foremost. How then can we help adoptees move from feeling unchosen to feeling chosen, from rejection to embrace? One way to begin is for the adoptive parent and the adopted child to connect at the point of mutual need and sometimes shared pain. Adoptees are allowed to mourn the biological parents they never knew; adoptive parents may mourn the biological child they never knew. Shared pain is also paralleled in the labels that are worn in life. The adoptee bears the label of "relinquished"; some adoptive parents (not all) bear the label of non-fecund, infertile, sterile, barren.

This honesty about mutual loss and pain facilitates the grief work in adoption by transforming the process into a mutual one. Sociologist David Kirk named this process one of "shared fate" and wrote about it in a book by that title:

> It has already been suggested that the parents' recall of their own deprivation and pain, worked through but not discarded, may provide an instrument for keeping open the channels of communication. The method of the recall

of pain may also enable the parents to throw in their lot with the child's and thereby let him [her] experience the reality of his [her] membership in the adoptive family.[13]

The shared pain in grief can possibly become a channel of shared grace. In other words, we can be honest about the losses involved in adoption while affirming God's activity in personal history. Perhaps Kate, whose story about her sister-in-law Liz concludes chapter 4, can best describe what a channel of shared grace might be:

"As I traveled to China and witnessed the miracle of adoption, I again had the overwhelming feeling that God was at work doing something powerful. I watched as God united a caring American woman, who longed for a child, with an exquisite Asian child, who longed for a mother. In a perfect world, all parents who want biological children would give birth to them and all parents who give birth to children would be able to take care of them. But we live in a fallen world where social structures make it impossible for some people to keep their children, and children are abandoned. We live in a fallen world where people who desire children and have love to give remain childless. A loving God steps into our suffering and does something new. God gives the gift of adoption."

Relinquishment: From Rejection to Embrace

Child relinquishment is an old custom. Relinquishment is letting go of, releasing, yielding a child; in some instances, it means abandonment. Relinquishment has been practiced from the earliest recorded days in pre-modern Europe and into early modern culture.[14] It continues today in, for example, China. Important for this book is the fact that it occurred, as well, during the time when the New Testament books that mention adoption—Romans, Ephesians, and Galatians—were written.

The early church fathers, such as Clement of Alexandria and Tertullian, were well aware of the widespread child abandonment practices in the New Testament era. Abandonment in the time of the early church typically meant simply leaving the child somewhere, often a public place; selling the child; or legally relegating authority to another family or institution.[15] Many of these abandoned children ended up as servants, slaves, or prostitutes. The historian John Boswell has traced the history of child abandonment and identifies a number of reasons behind parental abandonment, including illegitimacy, poverty, hunger, a physical deformity in the child, and the desire to make an offering to God. Boswell notes that the decision to abandon a child was not always an easy one. He describes one father agonizing between choosing to allow the starvation of several of his children or the sale of one of them for money to feed the others.[16] Some parents intended the best for their children in abandoning them, leaving infants in such public places as on the temple steps, in the hope the child would be found by someone of privilege.

Although child relinquishment is not new, the research surrounding the complexity of feelings that this practice evokes is relatively new. Some adoption researchers have noted the lifelong grieving of some children over the idea that they were given away or given up. Remember the story of Hannes in chapter 1? Hannes's pastor emphasized the idea of being accepted, taken up, or embraced by adoption before Hannes had had an opportunity to deal with the issue of grief. Consequently, Hannes was unable to travel emotionally from a place of primal rejection to a place where rejection is coupled with embrace, embrace of his valid grief over being given up and embrace also of the fact that he was accepted by loving others, his parents. We cannot ignore the context of a child's life as Hannes's pastor did. Grief must be sufficiently dealt with before the awareness of "gift" can be appropriated.

Expectant parents are caught up in such anticipatory excitement that it does not usually occur to them that there will likely be grief work ahead for them and the child they are adopting. Many agencies do not touch on this aspect of the adoption process at all. It is only through hearing the story of his or her acceptance into the family that a child begins to perceive that while she or he was embraced by the adoptive family, she or he was relinquished by another.

Adoption counselors and psychologists vary in their suggestions as to how and when adoptive parents should discuss adoption with their children and as to the depth of the grief process. One school of thought postpones the discussion of adoption until the child is in the latency period—that is, between the ages of five and seven—arguing that only then does a child have the inner strength to incorporate and cope with the information. Others recommend that the adoption process be heralded and discussed from the earliest moments, from the coming of the child into the family. All contemporary counselors agree, however, that children should be lovingly told of their adoption by their adoptive parents.

The sense of being given up by parents can be set in motion with the understanding of the dual dynamics (given up—accepted by), to create the movement of being given to, of being embraced. As Ronald Nydam has noted: "Extrafamilial adoption is first of all an experience of rejection, of not fitting into this world where one begins, of being dismissed, separated from origins, denied the basic rights of birth, and offered up to unasked-for adoptive parents. It is also the experience of being received, accepted, taken in by others."[17] Hopefully, the pain of being given *up* which connotes abandonment, can be ameliorated with the understanding that an adopted child is given *to* a welcoming family, a phrase implying loving intent.

Contemporary studies of birth mothers and fathers have found that they try to do what is in the best interest of their child. They seek to give their child, for example, a loving home with a parent or parents who are able to provide for them. Nonetheless, Nydam notes, "For some adopted children the pain of [birth] parent loss goes very deep. They believe, as some state documents put in writing, that they were 'abandoned to the world' and were, therefore, objects of adoption."[18] It is essential that adopted children be helped to understand that relinquishment can be tenderly undertaken.

Angela Herrell, a birth mother, has written of her loving gift in a publication for Bethany Christian Services: "I was seventeen years old and five months pregnant. One of the most common feelings among birthmothers is the feeling of loneliness. . . . God brought the right adoptive family to me." She requested a semi-open adoption, which involved meeting the adoptive family on two occasions before her son was born. Since the birth, she has stayed in touch with the parents through correspondence and has anonymously attended some of her son's ballgames.

She still has times of loneliness and grief, but believes she made the right decision for her child. "Certain times of the year are more difficult for me than others—especially since my son's birthday is so close to Christmas. Mother's Day is hard, too. There's grief, and I think that will always be there. On the other hand, my son makes me smile. All of the reasons I chose adoption have been fulfilled—he has great parents, a wonderful education at a private Christian school, and a happy life. I am really pleased."[19]

When possible, it is beneficial to tell adopted children how lovingly the plans for adoption were made. It is of utmost importance that adopted children be told of how expectantly they were awaited, how they grew to life in the hearts of their adoptive parents. As early as 1943, Florence Clothier, a physician involved in adoptions, wrote: "The adopted child, more even than the [biological] child, needs the security of a firm foundation in the love of the adopted parents. More than the [biological] child, he needs the deep reassurance that he is accepted and loved by his adopted parents. To protect himself from his basic anxiety, the adopted child may even create outrageous situations that will force his adopted parents to prove their love for him and their wish to have him for their own."[20]

At times, proving their love can make extraordinary and arduous demands on parents. At the time of our interview, Nan and Steve Brown had three adopted children: Sallie, twenty; Darryl, sixteen; and Allison, twelve. The two girls had had mild medical problems; Darryl, in contrast, had serious behavioral, academic, and interpersonal difficulties and forced his parents time and again to prove their love for him. They had adopted him at three and a half months from a private agency. Nan and Steve had regularly sought appropriate professional help for Darryl. Nan had been a special-needs teacher before she and Steve adopted; with the coming of their children, she had chosen to stay at home as a homemaker. As Darryl became increasingly more violent and physical, he screamed at Nan, kicked out windows, and eventually, in a fit of anger, broke his younger sister's arm. Nan had struggled to manage him at home, but at this point, the psychologist who was working with them recommended a Christian residential treatment program in another state. At the time of the interview, Darryl had been in the treatment program for fifteen months and was soon to come home. The Browns' faithfulness and patience had never flagged as Darryl time and again forced them to prove their love. Embracing both her earlier pain of childlessness as well as the children she believed God had given her, Nan had no regrets, and spoke with loving passion: "We love our kids, and we wouldn't exchange them for any others."

Thrice Born

The identity search, grief, and the fact of relinquishment can give the adoptee a sense of a double self. Author Betty Jane Lifton has written of her painful search for identity as an adopted daughter, using the phrase "twice born." Finding the need for a sense of origins more basic than the sex instinct, she uses terms such as *bastard*, *changeling*, and *dark twin* to refer to herself as a replacement for the legitimate, biological child who might have been born to her adoptive parents. Lifton's *Twice Born: Memoirs of an Adopted Daughter* is her search for her dual identity. It is nuanced with passive-aggressive anger toward her adoptive mother in particular, and eventually toward her biological mother, whom she locates in New York City. Although the distinguished Jungian analyst Helene Deutsch, who was treating Betty Jane, found her client's persistent need to search for her biological mother a neurotic need,[21] I would still like to use Betty Jane's unwavering and zealous mission to discover her dual identity in order to tie together the previously stated themes of identity development, grief, and relinquishment. I will also illustrate the impact of being twice, perhaps thrice born.

As part of her grief work, Betty Jane Lifton freely discloses her distaste for her adoptive mother, yet also recounts a story of her mother's love. During a large family party when Lifton was in her teens, she was upstairs dressing to go out with her friends. She accidentally shattered a full-length mirror and, stunned, found herself screaming, "Mother." Aunts and uncles rushed into the house to help. Betty Jane saw her hysterical and frightened mother stumbling up the stairs, her whole being absorbed in the disaster. "This kind of love," she later wrote, "is surely no less than one feels for a natural child. Fate in its perversity had paired us together. She was my mother and I was her daughter."[22] As her adoptive mother lay dying years later, Betty Jane came to terms with her second birth:

I hold her fragile hand which shakes like the quivering body of a wilted bird and know that she who raises the child is the mother. My childhood will fade with her, revive with her. As long as she lives, my image, fluctuating through various stages of development, is reflected in her eyes.[23]

Before her adoptive mother died, Betty Jane completed a successful search for her biological mother and came to a place of reconciliation with the one who gave her the first birth.

"I feel as if I'm always with you," her biological mother replied in a hushed voice, "because you are a part of me. Just knowing that your life has turned out well is enough for me. I feel I have no right to more."[24]

As the two births connected, the fragments of Lifton's life come together.

Her words—so warm and loving—threw into place so much of what I had been struggling with. We could never completely let go of each other. For a natural mother's child will always be a part of her, just as she will always be a part of her child.[25]

Lifton's life and her use of the phrase "twice born" illustrates for all of us in the adoption triad a unique aspect of the growing pains of adoptees, particularly as they move from adolescence into adulthood: the formation of identity that incorporates the issues of grief and relinquishment that I discussed earlier in this chapter. In her book *Lost and Found: The Adoption Experience*, Lifton uses and expands upon the idea of adoption as a metaphor for the human condition.[26] Each person, she argues, is on a mythic quest for connectedness to the world and to each other and engaged in a process that eventually reveals who we really are.

Who are we really? Lifton's phrase "twice born" is very similar to the phrase second birth. Christians claim connectedness to God and to each other through a "second birth" as described to Nicodemus in John 3:3:

Jesus answered [a Pharisee named Nicodemus], "Very truly, I tell you, no one can see the kingdom of God without being born from above."

Being born again by the Spirit of God has been described by many Christians as a second birth. Yet, adoptees like Lifton have made us aware that for them, what Jesus is describing is a third birth. We are, first, born by nature; second, born by nurture; third, born by spirit. In this third birth we find our true connectedness to our Creator, to each other, and to ourselves as adopted children of God.

An Unimagined Life

Clara Claiborne Park, cited at the beginning of this chapter, described a life with surprises as an "unimagined life." Parenting adopted children is not only filled with surprises, but with major pieces of missing information. That information can include significant parts of a child's medical history or heritage. The term "genealogically bewildered" has been applied to adoptees who lack information about their family tree. This information gap can leave parents and even medical authorities perplexed in the face of a medical or behavioral problem that has a genetic component.

Nan and Steve Brown faced just such an unknown medical problem with their twenty-year-old adopted daughter Sallie, who started to lose the hair on her head while, simultaneously, the hair on her arms turned very dark. Her metabolism slowed, and she gained weight. Sallie was eventually diagnosed with a genetic syndrome that manifests itself in the late teens and twenties. When the doctor found out Sallie was adopted, he said that had her history been known, the syndrome, which includes sterility, could have been prevented, although it has been arrested.

The hopeful note is that, increasingly, adoptive parents and adoptees are demanding and receiving full medical histories early in the adoption process. Open and semi-open adoptions provide easier access to medical and other hereditary records, which adoption activists today are calling the "civil rights" of the adoptee. These medical records should optimally include information about psychiatric conditions such as behavioral and mood disorders, psychotic disorders, psychoactive substance abuse disorders (drug and alcohol abuse), and organic mental disorders in the birth parents.

Some examples may help here. An unsuspecting and uninformed couple might adopt a newborn and deal with what they assume are simply the terrible twos and the terrible threes, only to discover their child's oppositional and reckless behavior never stops. They may over time be accused of improper parenting; of, for example, providing too little discipline, too much discipline, too few boundaries, too many restrictive boundaries, too little or too much spanking. If they express concern when their child engages in risk-taking behaviour, they may be accused by counselors or psychologists of being over-anxious, overprotective, or neurotic. (These labels are used more often for adoptive mothers than fathers, perpetuating the tendency in society to scape-goat women.) Without sufficient medical and genetic history, some disorders, including mental disorders, cannot be diagnosed in a timely manner by mental health practitioners or physicians. Prenatal drug exposure is often unknown. A child with ADHD or ADD, for example, may not be diagnosed until first or second grade. Since there is a 32–36 percent chance that male adoptees will have ADD and a 6–14 percent chance for female adoptees, it would be helpful for adoptive families to be alerted to a history of ADD in the birth family.[27] Similarly, a child with bipolar disorder (manic depression) cannot be diagnosed until approximately age thirteen. Thus, adoptive parents may witness acting-out behavior of varying sorts and may endure judgments or platitudes from observers ("You are not strict enough!" "Lay down the law." "Boys will be boys."), only to discover later that their child has an organic, hereditary condition.

The issue of the influence of biology versus the influence of environment in a person's development continues to be debated by theorists in various places on the nature vs. nurture spectrum. The lack of information regarding adoptees' genetic or biological background makes this debate even more difficult. The absence of information can be particularly acute in infant and international adoptions.

Only 2–3 percent of children in the U.S.A. are adopted. Yet 4–5 percent of children referred to outpatient mental health facilities are adopted. In residential care facilities, 10–15 percent are adopted children.[28] Adoptees in general have greater psychological vulnerability and a greater likelihood to display acting-out tendencies when problems arise.[29] At the same time, it is also true that adoptive parents are more likely to seek professional help. The home studies and counseling they have participated in through the adoption process give them an advantage and an openness in seeking appropriate assistance for their struggling child or teenager. They know there are missing pieces to the puzzles of their child's life and avail themselves of support systems in the best interest of their child.

It Takes a Church to Raise a Child

Many of the interviewees for this book commented on the faith and ecclesiastical resources that helped them raise their children. Prayer groups, Bible study groups, devoted friends and fellow parishioners, and pastors were mentioned as resources of faith. In the case of Nan and Steve Brown, whose son Darryl was in a residential treatment program, the church even helped pay for him to complete the program when the Browns' finances were low.

It takes a church to raise a child, to surround a family with an assembly of supporters and an array of resources. There are three specific areas in which the church can strive to create a stronger theological foundation around all the adoptees of God: (1) in the development of God-images; (2) in the reformation of self-image; (3) in the living praxis of the household of faith.

God-Images

The predominant image for God in mainline churches today is God the Father. We are familiar with this image of God from Scripture. It is quite natural that we infuse the image with emotional power and transfer our feelings from our earthly father onto God, for it is not only from Scripture that we know what a father is like; we know from experience. The adopted child has two fathers, actually a double set of parents or a "double representational world" of rejecting birth parents and accepting adoptive parents. This can affect and complicate the adoptee's image of God. Being given up by those who created you is a basic, or primal, rejection. The adoptee can feel rejection and deep anger about being relinquished and may project or aim this anger onto God, who is also a creator. Theological healing involves turning from the Rejecting God to the Embracing God so that the Rejecting God is seen as the Giving God. This change is accomplished not through a splitting—that is, by clearly separating parents into bad birth parents and good adoptive parents—but rather by understanding the birth parent as both relinquishing and giving. A parallel can be drawn with the Incarnation, where we can see a connection between lovingly giving and relinquishing:

For God so **loved** the world that [God] **gave** [God's] only Son. (John 3:16)

Whereas God as Father functions prominently in the Incarnation, the birth father is often invisible in the adoption process. Thus, one father figure is relinquishing, the other is absentee. As Ronald Nydam has observed:

Extrafamilial adoption may have a powerful impact on one's image of God. As with other forms of the human dilemma, extrafamilial adoption is one in which a human being—a *little* human being—may be at risk in terms of being sufficiently grasped by the gracious hand of God.[30]

The church has its theological work to do in augmenting its images of God. Early in the Westminster Confession of Faith (6.023), God is described as a birthing parent:

> After God had made all other creatures, he created man, male and female . . . after his own image.

In the next chapter, God leaves his children:

> The most wise, righteous, and gracious God, doth often-times leave for a season his own children to manifold temptations and the corruption of their own hearts. (6.028)

Scripture also reinforces the idea of a relinquishing parent. As cited earlier, a loving Father God relinquished a son for the love of the world (John 3:16, my paraphrase). From this Scripture alone, we can imagine how, in the mind of a *little* human being, a *little adopted* human being, love may be connected with godly relinquishment at best, with abandonment at worst. This awareness should surely beckon practical theologians, pastors, and Biblical exegetes into a reconsideration of the church's most popular image for God, God as Father.

We need a new image for God as Adopting Parent. If the church can develop the Christian anthropological view of a human being as "adopted child of God," then God can be viewed more centrally in our liturgy, preaching, and teaching as Adopting Parent as well as Birth Parent. How do we begin? Let's look at Scripture. The book of Ephesians is replete with family imagery.[31] It mentions children of wrath (2:3), children of light (5:8), God as adopting father (1:5), and a glorious inheritance (1:11, 14, 18). Of all these, the image of God that the church has neglected to uplift is that of Adopting Parent.

God as Adopting Parent forms a new family that Bruce Malina describes as "fictive brothers and sisters in Christ" in *The Social Gospel of Jesus: The Kingdom of God in Mediterranean Perspective*. By *fictive*, Malina means non-biological support groups that form associations such as house churches.[32] Whereas bloodlines and marriage constituted family groupings before, Jesus' social gospel crosses traditional lines. These radical new groups of "adoptees" included both circumcised Israelites and uncircumcised Greco/Romans. Malina noted:

> For a number of these Israelites, the acceptance of Jesus as Israel's Messiah led them to replace their relationships with their brothers and sisters in

Israel with a new relationship with brothers and sisters in Israel's Messiah, brothers and sisters in Christ.[33]

This emerging household of faith was essentially an adopted family.

Self-image: Rereading the Prodigal

The late Henri Nouwen wrote of his spiritual development in relation to the parable of the Prodigal Son and Rembrandt's theological and artistic depiction of the story (see chapter 5). The parable of the Prodigal Son is familiar to most churchgoers. It is traditionally read from the perspective of a biological father welcoming back his biological, wandering son. Nouwen reads it from three perspectives: the son, the father, and the elder brother. Yet, Nouwen develops the parable on the assumption that the son is physical progeny. But what if we discard our assumption that the parable is a story of family members connected by blood, and reread it as the story of an adoptive family? What insights might be gained? I believe this reading can inform our self-image as Christians, adopted to God. This rereading is also inclusive of families formed through adoption.

Jeff, vice-president of an academic institution on the east coast, is living a version of the parable. His anguished heart as an adopted father gives a glimpse of how very much God as Adoptive Father loves, suffers, and welcomes the wandering child.

Jeff

"When I received the news about adopting a son, I realized that my life was going to change forever. It was kind of scary." Jeff's was an agency adoption; his father was chair of the agency board. The five-month-old baby boy was healthy, but had been in two foster homes and had thus experienced early separations. Only very reluctantly did the baby let go of the foster mother, grabbing her necklace. Jeff remembers that the baby (Nick) looked at him and his wife, Linda, with detachment, which may have even that early indicated the beginning of what specialists call an "attachment disorder."

Two geographical moves later, son Nick continued to be playful but observant. A Caucasian, he went to a neighborhood school that was 80–90 percent African American. Elementary school went well; he made good grades effortlessly. Things began to change in middle school. In seventh grade, he asked to know more about his birth parents. He picked out another school for eighth grade, but he did not integrate well. Psychological problems emerged, and he was physically violent, wielding baseball bats and breaking windows; he ran away.

Jeff comments, "I've never felt helpless about anything. . . . I was in utter misery; he was in utter misery. We could not go on." At fifteen, Nick was sent to Montana for six weeks for a wilderness program. "That helped," Jeff recalled. "Then we tried a home-based behavior-modification program for two years involving us parents, the school counselor, the academic advisor, the Director of Christian Education at church. We had locks on the TV at home; everything was earned. We felt like we were living in a prison. At age sixteen, he spiraled down again. Again, he was sent to a wilderness school for two years, this time near our hometown." Nick later credited the wilderness school with saving his life. But Jeff cautions, "he was determined to do himself in one way or another." He completed high school, but began selling drugs. At nineteen, Nick dropped out of junior college and covered his body with tattoos. He took various jobs involving driving, then got four moving traffic violations.

Jeff laments, "This is an incredible story of a kid who is normal and bright but is so hung up about something that he is making all of these bad decisions consciously. I love him. I care about him. But I have had to build a firewall around my deep, most inner self, because if I dwelt on it it would make me so sad, I couldn't cope."

Jeff and Linda try to be non-judgmental regarding their son's appearance and choices. "We have a profound conviction that Nick was God's gift to us. We were called to give him a home. . . . For someone like me who has led a charmed life, to have some painful situation like this, always present, can be God's way of keeping us humble and dependent on God. You develop a profounder grasp of God's grace and providence."

"I gave Nick the beautiful Henri Nouwen book. I wrote on the first page: 'This is my story, too.' It is my story to the extent that we are all estranged from God in our fallen state. God chooses nonetheless to adopt us as God's children—an amazing grace. We don't know how desperate we are; we can't appreciate the doctrine of adoption."

Jeff's heart is broken. He is in a position of grief similar to Rembrandt's when he painted "The Prodigal Son." Rembrandt had over time buried his dear wife Saskia, three sons, and two daughters. The loss of his son Titus was particularly devastating. Nouwen described the soul of Rembrandt as that of a suffering father:

Created in the image of God, Rembrandt had come to discover through his long, painful struggle the true nature of that image. It is the image of a near-blind man crying tenderly, blessing his deeply wounded son. Rembrandt was the son, he became the father.[34]

In his book, Nouwen moves into all the positions in the Biblical account: the prodigal son, the judgmental elder brother, the welcoming father. He brings the reader graciously into all three characters. He fails, however, to reread the parable from the standpoint of the adoptive family, the family that is not biologically connected. And Nouwen himself missed an important point about Rembrandt's depiction of the scene of welcome. The Prodigal Son is not leaning against the chest of the father, as Nouwen has it; the returning renegade is pressed against the abdomen of the parent. This togetherness, this connectedness, this love in extremity, is the womb-love or tender compassion and mercy of God. Wherever we find ourselves in the parable of the Prodigal, the basis of our self-image is as Beloved of God.

Household of Faith

It takes a church to raise a child. Within this church, it takes Christian families willing to respond to the calling to adopt children who need them. In the introduction, I referred to a seminary family who responded to an old hymn titled "Here I Am, Lord" and felt called to adopt, over time, seven special-needs children. One of the seven children, Jacob, eighteen at the time, gave a sermon that ended with this song and its impact on the family. One line in particular summarized his transformed image of himself from an abused child in a violent home into a child of God in a household of faith. That line talks about God breaking hearts of stone and turning them into hearts for love alone.[35]

I would like to close with this sermon because it not only gives an adopted child the last word, it also illustrates the significance and importance of church members taking seriously what it means to be a household of faith. Jacob also contrasts a home of violence with a home of grace.

Jacob's Sermon

I want to focus on one Psalm for now. That is Psalm 27, which is my favorite chapter in the Bible. Again, David is talking about the Lord's protection over us. Even though your enemies may try to conquer you, or someone may want to pick a fight with you, or your co-workers don't like what you are doing, God will guide and protect you through those difficult times. For me, Psalm 27 means a lot. Whenever I read this chapter, I feel a sense of comfort and victory.

As some of you may already know, I was adopted at the age of six. My life before that was pretty hectic. It was a life that you would not want to live through. I was born on May 19, 1983, to parents that just were not ready for two twin boys. They were barely able to take care of themselves. . . . At the age of sixteen months, I had open-heart surgery. There was a hole about the size of a quarter in the interior wall of my heart. As bad as this may sound, open-heart surgery was the easiest event in my early life that I had to deal with. . . . In my birth records, it says I suffered a head concussion. I vaguely remember that, but Paul, my twin, had a flashback once. He pictured me being thrown against the wall by my birth father. . . . Whenever one of us would cry, our parents would give us baby bottles. But they were not filled with warm milk. Instead, they were filled with warm beer.

Both my parents had major drinking problems. . . . One day when my birth father was drunk . . . he took a hand-gun . . . and walked down the street shooting at parking meters. . . . There were many times when my birth mom, Paul, and I were in and out of shelters because of the behavior my birth father was displaying.

The drinking problem that my birth father had also led to the abuse that he displayed on all three of us. I can't remember details, but I do remember being both physically and sexually abused. . . . All this happened for three years until finally Paul and I were taken out of the home. We were placed in a foster home. We lived in this foster home for three years, in Oshkosh. These parents didn't have the drinking problems, and they didn't abuse us. In fact, they were awesome. After those three years, we were placed in another foster home in Green Bay. . . . We lived there for a few months until we were ready to be adopted by the parents we have now. Paul and I moved in with these parents at the age of six and we have been living here for the past twelve years.

I think the scariest event that Paul and I encounter now are flashbacks.

I believe the Lord guided us through all this time of trouble, just as he guided David through his time of trouble. Both Paul and I could be dead right now, and I believe God kept us alive for a purpose. In Ps. 27:10, it says, "If my father and mother forsake me, the LORD will take me up." So no matter what the situation is, the Lord will always be there for you just as He was always there for me. He was by my side when I was thrown against the wall. He was by my side when I had open-heart surgery. He was also by my side when I was making choices that led me down a rocky road. But through the help of Sunday school teachers, friends, parents, prayers, and the goodness of the Lord, I was able to get back on the right road. . . . In Psalm 27, I am reminded by David of the protection of the Lord.

I said earlier that every time I read Psalm 27, I feel a sense of comfort and victory. I feel this sense of comfort because I know that I won't have to go through all of that again. . . . Most importantly, I am grateful to have a family that cares about me and will help me through anything that comes along my way.

Our closing hymn is a song which means a lot to my parents. God used both of them to be there for kids who needed a loving home. We have seven adopted kids in our family, and my parents changed all of our cold hearts into warm, loving hearts. They were willing to give up what they had to be servants of the Lord. The Lord was looking for someone, and my parents said, "Here I am, Lord."

Please join me in singing our closing hymn #525, "Here I am, Lord."

Chapter 7

A Theology of Adoption

Some readers of the Good Friday story, in which Jesus dies, cheat, because, knowing the Easter outcome, they do not allow for Jesus' own sense of abandonment at the crucial stage.
Martin Marty, A Cry of Absence:
Reflections for the Winter of the Heart

*I*n the spring of 1995, a theological conversation developed in my seminary class on the topic "Family of Heart: A Theology and Psychology of Adoption." Attendees were adoptive parents, biological parents, and adult adoptees. Social workers, foster parents, and birth parents spoke to the class. Late in the semester, theological discourse occurred that I had never experienced in twenty-four years of teaching. The depth of our conversation was occasioned not only by personal histories, but also by both the pain and the healing that underlay the exchanges and interchanges. One seminarian's contribution invigorated another's, then another's. If communication can be communion, it was so.

In this theological communion, God's inclusive embrace held each person present. The primal wounds of adoption, the abandonment and rejection issues, the joy of homecoming, the love of a child, sacrifice and benevolence—all of these complicated aspects of adoption were recognized as part of God's own experience. It was as if each member held one pane of a stained glass window. We put the panes together to form an image in which we saw more of the fullness of God.

The focus began with God, First Person of the Trinity. Our emphasis was first on God as Creator; then we moved to God as the birthing parent, the birthing mother. The latter is a difficult image for some, because it is so unlike the more traditional and familiar images of God and of God's relationship to people, such as, king to kingdom, where the power of God is kinglike, dominating, controlling. In contrast, the power of a God who is Birthing Mother is lifegiving, generative, nurturing.[1] It is power emanating from the womb-love of God. In Scripture, God conceives (Isa. 42:14), suffers labor pains, births (Deut. 32:18), and nurses (Isa. 49:15) a child. God is depicted as birthing mother, midwife (Ps. 22:9–11), mother bear (Hos. 13:8), mother hen (Matt. 23:37), and mother eagle (Deut. 32:11–12). Numerous examples of God's mothering activities are sketched in Hos. 11:3–4; Is. 46:3–4; Isa. 66:13–14.

As feminist theologians have noted, the power coming from such a God as this is the power found in relationships.[2] Biblical scholar Phyllis Trible has developed the maternal metaphor of God as birthing mother by connecting two Hebrew words with the same root: *womb* (*rehem*) and the adjective *merciful* or compassionate (*rahum*). The word *rahum* is used exclusively for the Creator God, never for creatures. As Trible notes,

> When Yahweh is spoken of as "merciful and gracious" (Ps. 86:15; 111:4; 145:8; Neh. 9:17), this is the term that is used. . . . Given the frequency with which mention of God's merciful compassion appears in scripture, it can hardly be said that such female imagery is peripheral to the tradition even though, until recently, it has gone unnoticed.[3]

God's merciful compassion is God's womb-love.

Contemporary theologians have ignored the image of God as Adoptive Parent. This is especially problematic in light of passages such as Eph. 1:5, Rom. 8:15, and Gal. 4:4–5, which speak of God in this relational way. However, from the adopted child's point of view, at least according to the adult adoptees in the seminary class, the images of God, first person of the Trinity, as either birthing parent or adopting parent are personally, although not Biblically, problematic. The problem is that for them adoption was like an amputation. The wound of relinquishment left them with a sense of emptiness, abandonment, and alienation. Knowing that they'd been chosen by adopting parents revived the knowledge of being "unchosen" by birth parents. The poetess Sue Walker illustrates the wound of relinquishment in her poem "To Mama":

To Mama
(on my birthday)

Where are you, woman?
You who lay spread-eagled
Thirty years ago today
Casting out nine months of me

With a heave and a shove—
Do you remember?
For it was your delivery day.

Did you ever hold that kid of yours?
Take me in your arms?
Or was it an instant's separation
As quick as the snip of cord
That severed us two?

And now do you ever wonder like I do . . .
If my eyes are like yours?
Nearsighted? Lapis blue?
Are you thin like me?
And is the little finger on both your hands
Just a bit crooked like mine?

You have three grandsons;
Their eyes are blue; their hair is fair;
Two are twins almost three
But they call another Grandma
And I another, Mother.

One day I'll come
Traveling my shadow to your door.
"Collecting for the heart fund,"
I will tell you,
Take your dollar
And drive away.

Sue Walker
Mobile, Alabama[4]

At this seeming impasse around the pain of relinquishment, the students did their most profound theological work. They entered into God's woundedness and brought Christ into the adoption circle of faith. Their point of entry, I believe, was the aloneness of God, second person of the Trinity, in Gethsemane, the cry of abandonment on the cross, and the separation that ensued:

Then, in the soul's dark night and the heart's deep winter, comes the recall of a shriek or a groan more intense than all the others. The quotation on the cross comes from the psalms, and I can never let it go: *My God, my God, why hast thou forsaken me?*[5]

The adult adoptees connected Christ's cry of dereliction, "My God, my God, why have you forsaken me?" (Mark 15:34) at the crucifixion with the primal wounding of both the adoptee and relinquishing parents to develop a theological image of a God not only as Adopting Parent *but as* Relinquishing Parent and as Relinquished Child. The vulnerability of God would then include not only anxious yearning as Adoptive Parent, but pain as Relinquishing Parent and abandoned agony as Forsaken Child.

Divine Kinship

As part of his work in the class, Stephen Kolmetz, an adult adoptee, applied theological language to his faith journey.[6] Stephen constructed a theology by using his own experience as an adoptee as a lens by which to view Scripture, a means of interpretation or, in this case, "an adoptive hermeneutic." Through this lens of adoption, he was able to develop his understanding of both Christology and the doctrine of evil. For him, this was not a rational exercise; it was his life. Stephen has given me permission to cite the development of his thought from his paper, "The Cabbage Patch Gospel: Adoption and Spiritual/Theological Formation."

Stephen identified with Jesus' address of God as Abba in the Garden of Gethsemane. Abba is an intimate Aramaic term similar to our English word *Daddy* and is found three times in the New Testament: in Jesus' prayer in Gethsemane (Mark 14:36), in Rom. 8:15, and in Gal. 4:6. Romans and Galatians also use the Greek word *huiothesia*, which means "adoption." The image of God as mother caused primal memories of abandonment and rejection to resurface for Stephen. God as Father was a less threatening image to him, but as a parental image, it lacked the feminine dimension. Abba father offered a nurturing, caring divine parent. Yet, even with this connection to a caring parental God, something was missing. That something was the connection to his birth mother.

This missing connection is a consequence of evil—evil found neither in the practice of adoption nor in the act of relinquishment by the birth mother but rather in the unjust social systems and situations that force a mother to relinquish her child. Choosing the language of relinquishment rather than abandonment moves us away from blaming the birth mother, who is in many ways a victim herself.

Abandonment carries overtones of renouncement, desertion, dereliction. *Relinquishment*, in contrast, can include nuances of sacrifice, yielding or rendering up something beloved, relaxing one's hold on someone. As we reword and reframe the process of yielding up a child in love, the responsibility shifts toward the evil of a society that condemns an unwed mother and does not offer the financial and moral support she needs to raise the child. Nonetheless, Stephen insisted, "no change of language can erase the radical evil in the adoptee's separation from the birth mother."[7]

The wounding of adoptees that occurs because of separation from this most essential, symbiotic relationship is like the fall of humanity in the Genesis account of the Garden of Eden. The Garden is a "very womb-like place where there is an immanent connection between God and humanity much like the umbilical cord which connects the growing fetus to the mother. This Garden is a milieu of comfort, nurture, peace."[8] The intimate relationship is broken, however, and humanity is orphaned into the world. This severing of the first and most intimate of all relationships results in such a wounding that the loss permeates all of life.

Many adoptees want to seek, find, and connect with their birth parents. That is not always possible because earlier adoption files, at least, were typically closed by agencies. Stephen observed a parallel: "We want to reach out to our divine birth parent, but like adoptees whose files are closed, we cannot find God on our own. Fortunately, God as our birth parent did what we could not and sought us out."[9] In this way, God becomes both birth parent and adoptive parent.

This adoption occurs through the person and work of the Second Person of the Trinity who was without sin and primal woundedness. Christ understands the experience of the adoptee since he had no human father. Unlike the adoptee, however, he did not experience the wounding separation from his mother. As Stephen noted, Christ, like an adoptee, was different from those around him, and no one could truly understand his sufferings. "He was part of humanity but he was also not part of humanity, and therefore he experienced something of the adoptee's sense of belonging and yet not belonging to the family. . . . It was because Christ had no primal wound caused by separation from God that he could take upon himself the woundedness of all humanity and enter our abandonment and estrangement."[10] His cry from the cross, "My God, my God, why have you forsaken me?" becomes the point at which an adoptee knows that he/she is understood in their pain of separation. Through his resurrection, Jesus became the first to be adopted and reunited with his Abba, thus opening the process for all future adoptees like Stephen.

The hermeneutic or the "lens" of adoption allows us to see that adoption closely follows the Reformed doctrine of justification, putting us once again into an intimate relationship with God. Simultaneous with our adoption, we are reunited with our birth parent, God. Just as the reunion with a birth parent is transformative for adoptees, so reunion with God changes us. This process of change parallels the Reformed doctrine of sanctification. The relationship with God as Birth Parent matures as the woundedness of the adoptee moves toward healing by the work of the Holy Spirit, third person of the Trinity. Stephen describes the spiritual growing pains: "It is by the work of the Holy Spirit that we are being transformed into the full adoption of children of God which Christ models for us. . . . Like the resurrected Christ, we still bear our scars as reminders of who we were and who we are. Through our adoption in Christ the journey towards wholeness has begun."[11]

The Mutability of God

A theology adequate to undergird the adoption process must include both God's rejoicing and God's woundedness. If we view God as unchangeable (immutable) or incapable of suffering (impassible), the resulting theology will be insufficient to contain the passion and pathos felt by the adoptee. If, however, we view God as mutable (capable of change) and passible (capable of suffering), we open up possibilities of relationship to the adoptee. Philosopher William L. Power uses the word *omnipassable* in reference to God's receptivity to the world's influence.[12]

Theologian Cynthia L. Rigby summarizes the theological shift from an immutable to a mutable God from a trinitarian perspective of the cross:

> Seeking to understand what the cross reveals about the divine character, Reformed theologians have recently been talking about God as one who is vulnerable as well as omnipotent. . . . As we marvel that the God of the universe is cradled in the arms of Mary, as we witness the Holy Spirit's defiance of organizational efficiency, our contemporary understanding of what constitutes power is challenged to the core.[13]

God is vulnerable and capable of feeling and suffering. That is, God is passible. A Jewish legend preserved in the Talmud illustrates this: Rabbi Yoshua ben Levi asked of Elijah the Prophet when the Messiah would appear. Elijah, in response, encouraged the rabbi to ask the Messiah himself. How would the rabbi know him? Messiah was sitting among the poor at the gates of the city and was covered with wounds. Those other than the Messiah would uncover all their wounds at one time, then bind them all up again. The one who was Messiah unbound only one wound at a time so as to be ready when needed, so as not to delay for a moment his response to crisis and suffering. These actions of the Messiah were taken as a clue to God's identity—as *wounded healer,* ready with passion and pathos, both tending to his own wounds and prepared to tend to those of others.[14]

Some of those wounds that God unbinds are like those felt in the adoption process. For example, God participates in the woundedness of rejection. By virtue of the fall of humankind, God bears a primal or fundamental wound. Some theologians view this as an accidental property, not essential to who God is. Nevertheless, God has relinquished humankind in the fall. God has been rejected. God has known abandonment. This is true for both God the Father and God the Son. With this recognition, the adopted child has points of entry into the theological discourse about how to be at home in God's family. God was relinquished in the person of Christ to become the Firstborn of a new family, through which men and women could become adopted sons and daughters. There is divine pathos—that is, pity or compassion—in this; there is as surely joy in the homecoming. Both are needed to complete a theological circle of identification and discourse.

Theological discourse relies on the premise that God is not indifferent or unmoved by humankind. If that were the case, verses such as Ps. 86:15—"But you, O LORD, are a God merciful and gracious, slow to anger and abounding in steadfast love and faithfulness"—would be without context or content.

The theologian Nicholas Wolterstorff lost his son, age twenty-five, in a mountaineering accident. Until then Wolterstorff had interpreted the statement that no one beholds God's face and lives to mean no one survives after gazing on God's splendor. After his son's accident, when a friend suggested no one could see God's face of sorrow and live, Wolterstorff reflected that perhaps God's sorrow was God's splendor:

> For a long time I knew that God is not the impassive, unresponsive, unchanging being portrayed by the classical theologians. I knew of the pathos of God. I knew of God's response of delight and of his response of pleasure. But strangely, his suffering I never saw before. . . . Through the prism of my own tears I have seen a suffering God.[15]

From that, perhaps we can say that to develop a theology of adoption is to glimpse God's face and live. It is to glimpse the sorrow and the splendor of a Triune God who fully entered the adoption triad.

Diane: "I Call No Man Father"

The aloneness of Gethsemane and abandonment at Calvary are reflected in the story of Diane. The refrain that has accompanied me in the five years since I last saw Diane are these words of anger: "I call no man father."

Diane, a fifty-five-year-old Caucasian and married mother of three grown children, identified her problems as low self-esteem, pessimism, and a need for good coping skills. She described herself as becoming daily more dysfunctional, depressed, anxiety-ridden. She mentioned "panic attacks" and hypersomnia. Her bedroom became her cave.

During the four and a half years we met weekly, Diane experienced a number of crises and family events: the near fatal car accident of her daughter Holly, her husband's affair, the death of her father-in-law, the empty nest, the re-entry of two adult children back into the nest, daughter Holly's out-of-wedlock pregnancy, Holly's marriage, Holly's impending divorce, and sister Sarah's unemployment (Sarah had been helping Diane financially). Except for a probationary year at a bank and a temporary clerical position, Diane was unemployed for the four and a half years. Finances were a constant issue. Religion never was. Diane was Southern Baptist, but did not attend church or show any interest in Christianity.

Diane revealed little on her genogram (family history/tree). She would not talk about her biological father or her stepfather and repeated on several occasions, "I call no man father." She described herself as having had no power in her nuclear family, as being a "non-person." After one and a half years of weekly counseling, Diane acknowledged that she had been adopted as a newborn. The central theme of the counseling became her status as adoptee. Diane's birth father, married to her birth mother, gave her away in an informal adoption to their next-door neighbor. With a few sentences on scratch paper, Diane became the "daughter" of a single woman who, totally unprepared, made a bed for the infant out of a chest of drawers. Diane had an older sister who was not given away, and five more children were born to Diane's birth parents, all of whom were kept. Diane was the financial burden, the mouth that couldn't be fed.

During the years that Diane came for counseling, I became her adoptive mother. She transferred to me, as counselor, some of her feelings about her adoptive mother. This redirection of feelings from childhood is called a *transference* in therapeutic situations. Whether this transference predated my personal experience with adoption, was occasioned by it, or was strengthened by it, I do not know. However, the following story illustrates how it operated:

Diane's adoptive mother managed a convenience store, and Diane often stopped by the store on her way home from work, especially on afternoons when there was heavy rain, to rest a while and break the drive. Her adoptive mother would come to the screen door of the store while Diane stayed in her car outside by the gas pump. The mother would say, "I've been thinking about you." Diane would reply, "It's rough, Mom. It's been rough." Mother: "Yes, I know. I've been thinking about you." After a few minutes of emotional refueling, Diane would drive on, never leaving the car. I often felt she refueled in my office, as well, after saying in a variety of ways, "It's been rough." Although she was resistant to insight-oriented therapy that would have given her knowledge into her layers of feelings, Diane became somewhat open to supportive, expressive therapy. She had a difficult time reflecting on relationships, receiving interpretations, and expressing feelings.

We were making progress. One day, unfortunately, I made a mistake that had significant therapeutic consequences. I failed to tell Diane that the counseling offices were closed for Good Friday. She came and stood for a long time outside my door—my closed door. And I was not there. She scribbled a note of concern that something had happened to me. I discovered the note the following day. I had committed the unpardonable therapeutic sin, on Good Friday, of all times. I had forsaken Diane.

The next Friday, Diane announced that she had located her birth mother on the very afternoon I had "abandoned" her, Good Friday. I believe her anger with me freed her to search for her birth mother. Diane surprised her birth mother with a phone call, then a visit. The reunion was painful; her feelings toward her birth mother were ambivalent, at times hostile. "I didn't have any say when they rejected me from the family," she acknowledged. "I'm going to have a say this time. . . . I was helpless then, but I am not now. . . . I can take up for myself now. I couldn't then." Her birth mother, however, refused to mention Diane to her siblings, even though Diane desperately wanted to meet them.

When Diane said she felt "stuck," I asked her if she felt our sessions were helping her. She interpreted my question as a criticism that she was not doing more. Although I explained it was my attempt to make sure she was getting the support she needed, Diane heard rejection. When we explored possibilities about her rejoining the workforce to relieve both financial stress and depression, she interpreted this suggestion as collusion with her husband, daughters, and son. She saw them as trying to eject her from the family, a re-enactment of being given away earlier. The transference to me at that time was as birth father, the rejecting one. Diane left therapy. Remember: She calls no one father.

Diane's rage underlay her statement, "I call no man father." Her world view, perhaps her faith structure, was constructed around both this statement and the Golden Rule, "Do unto others as you would have them do unto you," which she often quoted when her birth mother did not respond as she hoped. Diane never talked about God, verbalized images of God, or talked in any way that could be traditionally construed as religious/spiritual.

"I call no man father." Sigmund Freud based what he called the "illusion" or wish-fulfillment of religion on the father-complex, the desire to have a father to protect us from helplessness. In contrast, in Diane's irreligious rage, I heard her aloneness. In Matt. 23:9, Jesus told the crowds and his disciples, "And call no one your father on earth, for you have one Father—the one in heaven." This injunction came in response to the hypocrisy and selfishness of the scribes and Pharisees and was followed by an angry passage in which Jesus calls, "Woe to you, scribes and Pharisees," whom he likens to blind guides. Their proselytes become "twice as much a child of hell" as themselves (23:15).

Children of hell. Diane's rage built as her newfound birth mother refused to acknowledge her with birthday cards and calls to the extent Diane desired. Embarrassed, her birth mother did not want Diane's siblings to know of her existence. Once again, Diane was excluded and rejected from her biological family.

The Biblical metaphor of adoption is one of inclusion and acceptance in the family of God. The image of God's adoptive family gives a counselor or pastor a theological foundation. The counseling space becomes a "holding environment" or secure place for those in the adoption triad. A holding environment in which one feels accepted may be exactly what an adoptee like Diane seeks.

While this metaphor of adoption is not meant to circumvent the grief work or the primal wounding we have discussed, it can point to the tormented heart of God, aching for the child alone in her Gethsemane, anguished over her cry of dereliction, seeking out the children of hell, the children of wrath, waiting for Diane to come home.

The Inclusive Family

Shortly before he died, the New Testament scholar Bo Reicke was reworking his approach to Ephesians, moving away from the commonly held idea that the first three chapters, which are doctrinal and abstract, are the key to the letter. In his revision, Reicke was going to assert that the last three chapters, filled with practical application, were the heart of the book.[16] Chapters 4–6 are filled with advice and admonitions about how to live and love as family of faith: Children of disobedience and wrath are to walk as children of light. Specific instructions are given as to how "beloved children" relate to one another. Household codes (rules of conduct) are offered in chapters 5 and 6.

Why are these practical chapters the heart of the book? Because they reveal how to live as adopted children of God. Eph. 4–6 develops the doctrine of adoption that is presented in the first three chapters. They are not only about how to live as Christians; they tell us how an adopted family functions. For example, Eph. 4:11–13 develops the theme of acceptance-of-differences, which is an essential theme in healthy adoptive families; the passage elaborates on this theme by advocating an acceptance-of-differences-of-gifts given by Christ for ministry. To illustrate this theme, in Eph. 4:15–16 an image is developed of the various parts of the body. The body comprises different limbs, organs, and systems, but it is the very difference that makes the body truly functional. Eph. 5:1 contains an exhortation to be as "beloved children" as Christians in Ephesus. This injunction was not given to flesh-and-blood siblings, but rather to the diversified followers of Christ who were forming a family by faith. In chapter 8 of this book, I develop this perspective further.

To read Scripture and highlight the passages on adoption is to read it through a different lens. It is the same when we read the parable of the Prodigal Son as the returning of an adoptive son to an adoptive family. The fact that we always assume the family is biologically knit reveals our prejudice in favor of biological "seed" and our elevation of physical progeny. It is to miss the family of faith.

A New Name

In the Old Testament, naming was a way of showing both ownership and belonging. To "surname" someone implied ownership. For example, when Joseph entered the household of Pharaoh in Egypt, he was given a new name (Gen. 41:45).

In modern adoption, the naming process gives the adoptive parent(s) a sense of connectedness to the child and has the intent of giving the child a sense of belonging. When the adopted child reaches a certain age, often in adolescence, the process of identity consolidation is primary. Some adoptees want to know their birth name, which is, more often than not, different from the name given by the adopting family. In some families, the issue of a name can become a crisis.

The issue of naming arose in the family of sociologist David Kirk. He and his wife, Ruth, had adopted several children. Kirk describes a shift in identity within his adoptive family that is instructive for those within the Christian family. During the year of a move from California to Montreal, their eleven-year-old son Peter began asking numerous questions about his adoption, his origin, his birth mother. Kirk realized in retrospect that Peter was understandably unsettled by the geographical move and the loss of friends.

However, one remark of Peter's startled the family. Peter said, "When I'm older, I'll change my name to hers [his birth mother's]."

It is in David Kirk's response to his adopted son that I see a message and a model for the church, the family of God. Kirk replied, "A name is a very personal possession. The name you had before you came to our family was taken from you without you having had any say in the matter. But a name is also a way of saying where we belong. So, if you should decide to change your name when you are grown up, and if I'm alive then, I will add your new name to our family name so that all of us can continue to belong together."[17]

Before this exchange, Peter had become inattentive at school, sometimes playing hooky. He had been irritable at home. After this conversation, his attitude underwent a noticeable shift. He applied himself at school and became more agreeable at home. Some weeks later, while father and son were playing handball, David Kirk called out half in jest to his son, "You know what— I'm getting ready to change my name." Peter's laughing retort: "That won't be necessary now."

To have someone love you enough to change their name on your behalf, not for reasons of property, or marriage, or status, or legality, but to draw claim on kinship, to effect a primal connection, is what an adopted child like Peter needs to hear to feel the bonds within the family. When Christians take the name *adopted children* of God, they are saying to those who have been legally and literally adopted: I will add your name to my name so that all of us can be seen to belong together, at home in God's family.

Chapter 8

A Biblical Embrace

*And when He [Christ] has finished judging all, He will summon us,
too: "You, too, come forth," He will say, "Come forth, you drunkards;
come forth, you weaklings; come forth, you shameless ones!" And we
will all come forth unashamed. And we will stand before Him, and He
will say: "You are swine, made in the image of the Beast, with his seal
upon you: but you, too, come unto me!" And the wise and the clever
will cry out: "Lord! why dost thou receive these men?" And He will
say: "I receive them, O wise and clever ones, because not one among
them considered himself worthy of this." . . . And He will stretch out
His hands unto us, and we will fall down before Him and weep . . .
and we will understand everything.*

Marmeladov, in
Crime and Punishment *by*
Fyodor Dostoyevsky

Esther: Adoptee and Advocate

Adoptees look for role models and often have an intuitive rapport with other
adoptees. There are eminent adoptees in the Scriptures with whom they can
connect. Christ himself was prefigured or "pictured beforehand" by one
prominent biblical figure, Moses, who became the adopted son of Pharaoh's
daughter. Scholars have spoken of Christ as the prophet-like-Moses whose
actions to liberate the Hebrew people from bondage have been seen by
theologians as a prefiguration of the work of Christ as Redeemer. Liberation
theologians, in particular, have described Moses as Liberator and the cross-
ing of the Red Sea as a paradigm for the deliverance of oppressed people.

If Christ as Firstborn of the Adopted Family is prefigured in the liberator
Moses, Christ as Advocate is also pretypified as in the defender Esther,

adopted daughter of Mordecai. Esther's boldness to advocate for her people, the Jews, was at the risk of her life.

Esther, on Mordecai's advice, concealed her Jewish identity when she was taken into the harem of King Ahasuerus, and after she was crowned queen. Mordecai discovered an assassination plot to kill King Ahasuerus and revealed it in time to save the king. Mordecai's name was recorded in the book of annals. Meanwhile, Haman rose in power and set out to destroy the Jews. Mordecai, a Jew, refused to bow down in obeisance to Haman, now an important aide and administrator to the king. Haman was furious, and in revenge, set out to destroy the people of Mordecai, the Jews, throughout the empire of Ahasuerus. He manipulated the king to decree that Jews, young and old, men and women, would be annihilated on the thirteenth day of the twelfth month. Mordecai was distraught, put on sackcloth and ashes, and sat before the king's gate.

Although the penalty for entering the inner court of the king unsummoned could be death, Mordecai advised Esther to go before the king:

> "For if you keep silence at such a time as this, relief and deliverance will rise for the Jews from another quarter, but you and your father's family will perish. Who knows? Perhaps you have come to royal dignity for just such a time as this." (Esth. 4:14)

Esther approached the king who favored her, the death penalty was not inflicted, and, instead, the king asked for her request. Esther invited the king and Haman to dinner on two occasions, gaining their confidence. At the second banquet, the king asked Esther to make a request, even to the half of his kingdom. She pleaded for the life of her people, stating that an enemy sought to annihilate them. The king promised to spare her life and that of her people. When the king asked who this enemy of her people was, Esther pointed to Haman, who was subsequently hanged and whose plot was averted.

The day of deliverance is still celebrated today as the feast of Purim. Esther, adoptee, in her role as advocate and deliverer pretypifies Christ by helping us imagine beforehand his role as advocate and deliverer.

Women who are adopted need such a role model as Esther. If adopted children are marginalized by the dominance of biologically established families, female adopted children are at double risk for discrimination. Women still have fewer role models in history and in culture.

Why would scribes and scholars develop so much biblical imagery around Moses and not around Esther? Three issues, I believe, have contributed to Esther's obscurity in comparison to Moses. The first area is her suitability as a model, the second revolves around her adoptive status, and the third is the factuality of her life.

Regarding the first issue, Esther's suitability as a model, we must note that neither she *nor* Moses were without flaws. Moses killed an Egyptian; Esther's final request of King Ahasuerus for the Jews in Susa resulted in the deaths of three hundred people. Moses was punished by God for disobedience; Esther has been discounted by some feminist commentators for her sexual compliance to King Ahasuerus.[1] Regardless of her possible imperfections, Esther, like Moses, can depict in part a role that Christ as Advocate would later effect without flaw.

Second, there is a lack of clarity about Esther's adoption. In the days of Ahasuerus (Xerxes I, 485–464 B.C.), a Hebrew named Mordecai, a Benjamite, raised Esther or Hadassah, his cousin, when her father and mother died: "Mordecai adopted [took] her as his own daughter" (Esth. 2:7).[2] Nonetheless, according to Jon D. Levenson, Professor of Jewish Studies, "It is not known what rules or expectations governed Mordecai's adoption of his orphaned cousin (2:7), for neither the Hebrew Bible nor even the massive legal canon of rabbinic Judaism provides for adoption (although the rabbis do warmly commend one who raises another's child)."[3] In other words, there are no laws or codes to formalize or "legalize" adoption as a procedure. This in no way discounts the informal adoption of Moses (Exod. 2:10), of Joseph's sons (Gen. 48:5–6), or of Esther. In fact, James M. Scott argues for the existence of "a demonstrable Adoption Formula" in 2 Sam. 7:14, the Davidic promise of divine adoption: "I will be a father to him, and he shall be a son to me."[4]

In the case of Esther, some scholars doubt whether the events of her adoption really occurred. Others, such as Sidnie White Crawford, view the book of Esther as "historical fiction",[5] aspects of truth embedded in a legendary adventure story. In short, there are differing views as to the historical accuracy of the book of Esther. However, Katheryn Pfisterer Darr offers the predominant perspective among scholars: "The rabbis believed that the book of Esther was a factual account of actual events that happened to real people."[6] Regardless of these debates, Esther stands as a prominent adoptee in the canon of Scripture. One can hope that in the future the church will teach more and preach more about Christ, a defender-like-Esther.

Anatomy Is Not Destiny

Adoption offers a counterbalance to a recurrent theme throughout the Old Testament, which is the essentiality of man's "seed," or biological descendants, to preserve and immortalize a family lineage. In a subtle way, the Hebrew Scriptures emphasize biological destiny. God said to Adam and Eve in the story of creation: "Be fruitful and multiply" (Gen. 1:28). From that account of creation until the time of Elizabeth and Zachariah, there is a constant expectation for sons to be born, for thereby the line of Abraham, Isaac, and Jacob is perpetuated. According to Jon Levenson, Professor of Jewish Studies, "generational continuity" or the birth of offspring is, for Jews, the equivalent of life after death, for the Hebrew Bible has no doctrine of the resurrection of the dead. In ancient Israel, death is tragic, final, and universal. In the book of Genesis, according to Levenson, "infertility and the loss of children (which have connections to famine and exile) are the rough functional equivalent of death, and miraculous birth is the functional equivalent of resurrection."[7] The matriarchs like Sarah and Rachel long for sons, even resorting to culturally approved surrogate means to obtain heirs [Sarah and her Egyptian maid Hagar, who bore Ishmael; Rachel and her maid Bilhah, who bore Dan and Naphtali]. A male heir symbolized God's blessing, evidence of God's covenant to Abraham. The Old Testament reads as a Hebrew family album of biological descendants. A reader might be led to the conclusion that biology or anatomy appears to be destiny.

Many cultures elevate the role of biology through physical progeny, especially male heirs. The Christian church often appears at a loss to offer a corrective. Ministry in general and pastoral care in particular has been influenced by this biological emphasis in the Old Testament as well as by the fields of psychology and psychiatry, which have afforded helpful insights into the behavior and cognitive tendencies of humankind. These areas of the social/behavioral sciences as well as pastoral care have been greatly impacted by classical psychoanalysis as developed by Sigmund Freud. Freud went so far as to state, "anatomy is destiny"[8] in 1912, and he presented the body and its mechanisms in addition to one's gender as determinative of a person's development. The male was the superior creation. According to Peter Gay, renowned biographer of Freud:

> By the early 1920s, Freud seemed to have adopted the position that the little girl is a failed boy, the grown woman a kind of castrated man. . . . Man, then, the male, was Freud's measure. By this time Freud had abandoned his earlier manner of treating the sexual development of girls and boys as parallel. Varying Napoleon's famous saying about politics, he offered a provocative aphorism: "Anatomy is destiny." The most obvious evidence for that destiny, he thought, is the observable distinction between boys' and girls' genitalia.[9]

Although theologians do offer discrepancies and variations in their assessment of Freud's contributions,[10] the consensus is certainly that Freud regarded reality as outside the realm of faith.[11] Freud remains to this day one of history's most ardent critics of religion. To him, religion was a sophistication of infantile wishes based on the pleasure principle of childhood. Reality was, for Freud, grounded in the physical world of anatomy, sexuality, and eroticism. Psychiatrist and psychoanalyst Harold Kelman concluded, "As a male genius, Freud evolved a male-oriented psychology, which he based on anatomic immutables—'anatomy is destiny'—buttressed by the canons and methodologies of nineteenth-century science."[12]

To what can we trace Freud's emphasis on biology? The Freud family Bible records that Sigmund (Sigismund) "entered the Jewish covenant" a week after his birth on May 13, 1856.[13] Sigmund's father Jacob was never ashamed of his Jewishness, even in a time of anti-Semitism, and read the Hebrew Bible at home in Hebrew.[14] "The young Freud acquired an enduring fascination with 'biblical history,' that is to say, the Old Testament."[15] We can surmise that Sigmund Freud was sensitive to the roles of biology and ancestry for two reasons: the anti-Semitism that was rising on the continent of Europe in his lifetime and the importance of the Hebrew lineage or "seed" in the Hebrew Scriptures. It is not surprising that an essential underpinning of classical psychoanalysis is the Freudian supposition that "anatomy is destiny." Freud's tendency to biologic determinism was concerned primarily with the importance of biology to personality and neuropathology, and he was scornful of religion. Nonetheless, Freud had been exposed to a biblical theology in the Hebrew Bible, and its influence can be found in his theory. And in turn, ministry and pastoral care inherit both the strains of biologic determinism from his psychoanalytic thought and a predisposition to elevate ancestry and lineage from the Hebrew Bible.

Does the New Testament continue the emphasis on biological heritage? It is in Matthew, the New Testament book that contains the genealogy of Jesus Christ, son of David, son of Abraham, that we find *both the genetic continuity and the radical discontinuity* with this male Hebrew lineage. Embedded in the list of patriarchs are five unlikely women: Tamar, a "childless widow" wronged by Judah; Rahab, a Canaanite prostitute; Ruth, a Moabite widow; Bathsheba, taken in adultery by David; and Mary, an unwed mother. Tamar, Rahab, Ruth, and Bathsheba are supporting players to the cast of fathers in the genealogy. Mary, however, introduces the radical discontinuity. How? It comes with

Joseph the husband of Mary, of whom Jesus was born, who is called the Messiah. So all the generations from Abraham to David are fourteen generations; and from David to the deportation to Babylon, fourteen generations; and from the deportation to Babylon to the Messiah, fourteen generations. (Matt. 1:16–17)

The birth of Christ is explained in such a way here that Mary *alone* is the biological parent. The Davidic genealogy ends with Joseph, the adoptive parent. Thus, Scripture's first family—Mary and Joseph—alter the bio-logic flow of lineage and inaugurate the Christian era. This first family represents a theological typology of the Christian household of faith—that is, a relationship based on the person of Christ, conceived by the Holy Spirit. For those in that lineage, *belief* determines one's inclusion as child of God.

Children of Promise

The concept of adoption is both a key to this Christian lineage and a clue to some of the more enigmatic passages in the letters attributed to Paul.[16] For example, in Gal. 4, there is a rather perplexing allegory or symbolic depiction of two women from Gen. 21 (Hagar and Sarah) and two covenants.[17] This allegory, used to show what baptism into Christ looks like, is however puzzling and subject to numerous interpretations:

> Now this is an allegory: these women are two covenants. One woman, in fact, is Hagar from Mount Sinai, bearing children for slavery. Now Hagar is Mount Sinai in Arabia and corresponds to the present Jerusalem, for she is in slavery with her children. But the other woman corresponds to the Jeru-salem above; she is free, and she is our mother. . . . Now you, my friends, are children of the promise. (Gal. 4:24–26, 28)

In allegory, concrete events and actual people are taken as the surface layer of deeper, hidden strata of truths. One woman in the allegory is Hagar, Egypt-ian slave, mistress of Abraham, mother of Ishmael. Hagar bears "children for slavery" (v. 25) and is represented by the law or Mt. Sinai from which the Ten Commandments came. She corresponds to the "present Jerusalem" (v. 25), in the time of apostle Paul, ca. 55 A.D., and is described as in "slavery with her children."[18]

The other woman in the allegory is Sarah, wife of Abraham, who after years of infertility bore Isaac at age ninety-nine and became a mother of nations as a Hebrew. She is portrayed in Paul's allegory as corresponding to the "Jerusalem above" (v. 26), that is, the church, and is portrayed as the mother of the children of promise. When depicted in linear fashion, the flow is as follows:

Hagar, slave (law) (4:24)   Sarah, free
    ↓   ↓
Mt. Sinai, children of slavery (4:24)   children of promise
    ↓   ↓
present Jerusalem (4:25)   Jerusalem above (church) as mother
    ↓
Christ, born under the law,
   born of woman (Mary) (4:4) ⟍ ⟋ (Gal. 4:5)

Paul, the author of Galatians, set up this allegory[19] to address the question whether a non-Jew must be circumcised, a procedure altering male genitalia. Circumcision was one of the volatile issues that divided Jews and non-Jews as they struggled to be "at home in God's family" in the churches of Galatia in central Asia Minor. As Pheme Perkins notes, "Had it been possible to aid the apostle by doing so, the Galatians would have expressed their gratitude for God's salvation with a gesture even more bloody and extreme than the castrated devotees of the local mother goddess cult."[20]

Into this divisive rendition of "male anatomy is destiny," Paul offers an allegory constructed around three women and their offspring. In the allegory, Sarah is a symbol for the Hebrew people, the children of promise, whereas Hagar represents those who are children of slavery. Paul shocks the reader by placing Christ, a Jew, born of Mary, under the law represented by Hagar (v. 4:4). As biblical theologian J. Louis Martyn puts it:

> God has elected to invade the realm of the wrong—'the present evil age' (1:4)—by sending God's Son and the Spirit of the Son into it from the outside (4:4–6). . . . Galatians is a particularly clear witness to one of Paul's basic convictions: the gospel is not about human movement into blessedness (religion); it is about God's liberating invasion of the cosmos (theology).[21]

This liberating movement occurs within this passage (Gal. 4:4–7, 21–31) through the mechanism of adoption. The blended household of God occurs through the process and the spirit of adoption. Children of the slave Hagar are adopted by Christ and become children of promise, heirs, sons, and daughters of the free woman [Sarah]. Christ alone has the versatility to cross family lines and bring the children of Hagar, who represent non-Jews, into the lineage of Sarah, whose offspring are Jews and the children of promise.

> But when the fullness of time had come, God sent his Son, born of a woman, born under the law, in order to redeem those who were under the law, so that we might receive adoption as children. (Gal. 4:4–5)

This coupling of Sarah and Hagar in the allegory is not meant to take away from the fact that Jesus was Jewish; the allegory extends the possibility for others to be included in a family of fictive kinship.

How can we all be on equal footing within the blended household of faith, at home in God's family? The idea of equality in the church can be found in the emancipatory verses:

> As many of you as were baptized into Christ have clothed yourselves with Christ. There is no longer Jew or Greek, there is no longer slave or free, there is no longer male and female; for all of you are one in Christ Jesus. (Gal. 3:27, 28)

This emancipation is dependent on the Liberator, Christ himself, who is described earlier as being born under the law. Adoption is the process that explains how Gal. 3:28 is accomplished.

In the story of the two women who bore sons to Abraham—Hagar and Sarah (Gen. 21)—reconciliation comes with another son, born of a woman (Mary). Jesus' story is a narrative of matrilineal descent, and it subtly juxtaposes itself against the background of the patriarchs: Abraham, Isaac, Jacob, Joseph. The juxtaposition of Mary and Joseph in the birth narratives and Hagar and Sarah in the Galatians allegory may be one way of illustrating the Christian view that there is neither male nor female, slave nor free, Greek nor Jew in Christ.

Richard Hays has identified a "logic of reversal" in the text of Gal. 3:1–14 as the blessing of Abraham comes to the Gentiles and in 4:21–31 as slaves become free:

> If God is a God who reaches out to call those who are not [God's] people, if God causes the barren to sing by granting children where they are least to be expected, then the inclusion of the Gentiles as recipients of the promise to Abraham is an act thoroughly consistent with the character and purposes of the God to whom prophetic Scripture bears witness.[22]

A logic of reversal is a mental calculation that makes sense based on consistent opposition to reason in light of the faithful character of God. Hays's logic of reversal can be taken one step further: Christ, while the seed and promise of Abraham, is born of woman (Mary), born *under the law (Hagar)* (4:5, my emphasis). Thus, in the allegory created by Paul to sketch what baptism into Christ looks like, Christ is aligned with Hagar. The process by which this baptism and oneness in Christ is effected is adoption. The ultimate logic of reversal is that the One who was the fulfillment of the law chose to be born

under the law, so that all might receive adoption as sons and daughters and become children of promise.

The illustration above is titled "The Procession of the Baptized to the Cross under the Midwifery of the Church." Through baptism into Christ, Sarah's and Hagar's previously divided children become adopted children. As the singular procession now winds its way into the Jerusalem above, the crucified Christ looms above the process. The woman of whom Christ was born welcomes the pilgrims, led by the women who were witnesses to the resurrection.

The family tree is altered. Whereas the language and lineage of the ruling families in Scripture have been dominated by sperm and seed of the patriarchs, Christ as the one seed *(sperma)* or offspring of Abraham (Gal. 3:16) has created a multiracial, diverse-strata, and cross-gender family of promise. A main point of discussion in the churches in Galatia had been whether there was a need for circumcision or physical alteration of the male genitalia. In pointing to Christ as the theological foundation of the church, Paul reminds the church that neither seed, sperm, circumcision, nor the male anatomy that makes them possible determine the destiny of humankind.

An adoptive family is aware that it is not secured by biological ties; there can be no expectation of physical similarity or genetic sameness. In similar fashion, the church as a healthy adoptive family moves into acceptance-of-differences of its adopted children of promise, children whose belief in God is their destiny.

The Spirit of Adoption

Both Romans and Ephesians offer insights into the spirit of adoption. Although there is mention of adoption in Gal. 4:5 and an adoption formula in 2 Cor. 6:18, the majority of the insight into being "at home in God's household" is in Romans and Ephesians.

Romans

The letter to the Romans offers a contrast between the children of the Spirit [of God] and the children of the flesh. Children of the Spirit are adopted as sons and daughters and become heirs with Christ. Children of the flesh resist adoption. As in the legal adoption process of today, there is a waiting period, according to Romans, before the full adoption is completed. Suffering is to be expected with adoption, as those adopted become heirs with Christ who suffers (Rom. 8:17). Yet the suffering is outweighed by the glory of the finalization of the adoption.

> For you did not receive a spirit of slavery to fall back into fear, but you have received a spirit of adoption. When we cry "Abba! Father!" it is that very Spirit bearing witness with our spirit that we are children of God, and if children, then heirs, heirs of God and joint heirs with Christ—if, in fact, we suffer with him so that we may also be glorified with him. (Rom. 8:15–17)

There is a tendency in contemporary culture to romanticize the legal process of adoption.[23] The Scriptures also veer away from this idealization of what it means to be adopted as an heir with Christ. Romans is inclusive of both the suffering and the glory:

> We know that the whole creation has been groaning in labor pains until now; and not only the creation, but we ourselves, who have the first fruits of the Spirit, groan inwardly while we wait for adoption, the redemption of our bodies. (Rom. 8:22, 23)

Hope holds out for this final adoption.

Paul's literary devices of contrast and parallelism, which I noted above (children of the Spirit/children of the flesh), are coextended to the parallel and contrast between adoption in the ruling dynasty in the Roman Empire (Julio-Claudian) and adoption in the household of faith. Most biblical scholarship to date has focused on the use of the word *huiothesia* (adoption) in the books of Galatians (ca. A.D. 55) and Romans (A.D. 54–58), both of which, it is generally agreed, were written by Paul. During the period of their writing, Nero ruled the Julio-Claudian Dynasty. Nero was both Claudius's stepson, through Claudius's fourth marriage to Julia Agrippina, and Claudius's nephew. Although Claudius had a biological son by Julia Agrippina, he adopted Nero at age twelve and made him heir to the dynasty. As I mentioned in chapter 2, adoption was an accepted and high-profile method of perpetuating a lineage. Paul would have been keenly aware of the role of adoption in the Roman world at the time of his writings and missionary travels, and he used this widely understood cultural process to illustrate the formation of a spiritual family. However, as E. Elizabeth Johnson emphasizes, God's impartiality in dealing with Jew and Gentile should "never be construed as reneging on God's promises to Israel."[24]

Paul's theological emphasis on adoption in Galatians and Romans is accentuated by the literary device of contrast and by his understanding of conversion. His own life contains an example of contrast and conversion: Paul was formerly called Saul and known as a persecutor of Christians. After he converted to become a follower of Christ, his name became Paul, the apostle, a defender of Christians.

Ephesians

The book of Ephesians contains the fullest scriptural treatment of adoption. Because scholars have focused on other issues such as authorship—Was the author Paul? A student of Paul? Another writer after the time of Paul?—the material on adoption in Ephesians has not been in the forefront of discussion, even though in Eph. 1, the doctrine of adoption is developed quite extensively. Although some scholars have connected the theme of adoption to Christology, the study of the person and work of Christ, I will examine the doctrine of adoption as it impacts ecclesiology, the study of the life of the church and the church's practices of faith and ritual.

Eph. 3:14–15 reads "I bow my knees before the Father, from whom every family in heaven and on earth takes its name." Roman subjects were expected to bow before the Divine Father of the Roman Empire, the Emperor. Statements like Eph. 3:14–15 show why Christianity was regarded by many to be a "disruptive social phenomenon and a danger to the security of the Roman state."[25] It is clear from Eph. 5:21–6:9 that the author of Ephesians showed no disposition to tamper with the basic familial structure of ancient society, which included *paterfamilias* or the father as head of the extended family.[26] Household codes or stylized rules of conduct are found in Eph. 5 and elsewhere in the New Testament. The household codes (*Haustafel*) contain ways of relating within various groupings: husbands/wives; masters/slaves; parents/children. The groupings traditionally contain culturally dominant groups such as husbands, masters, and parents. However, the pivotal verse (5:21), which introduces the groupings in the household codes, advocates mutual submission.

The author of Ephesians subtly develops another form of subjection to God as Divine Father, which supersedes the power of both the emperor, the Divine Father of the Holy Roman Empire, and the male heads or fathers of Roman households. As church historian Mary Rose D'Angelo observes, appeal to and resistance to Roman claims about family values were not mutually exclusive in the discourse of the earliest Christian communities.[27] However, for these earliest communities, the power of *paterfamilias* shifted: "I bow my knees before the Father, from whom every family in heaven and on earth derives its name." (Eph. 3:14, 15) The ultimate allegiance of loyalty is not to the Divine Father of the Holy Roman Empire (such as Nero), nor to the father of a Roman household unit, but to God as progenitor of a family secured by the spirit of adoption.

In the secular culture of the first and second centuries, a young man of eighteen and a girl of twelve and a half could marry, and could be engaged much earlier. Marriage was normally arranged by the will of the father(s). Roman legal texts show the importance of economic considerations to these arranged marriages. An engagement or betrothal was often dominated by the concept of earnest (money or other gift) paid by the bridegroom (or betrothed man) to the bride (betrothed woman). The earnest money was called *arra (arrha)* and derives from the same root as the Greek word for earnest or guarantee found in Eph. 1:14 (*arrabon*).

In a similar way, to Christians, the Holy Spirit becomes the earnest, or guarantee, of inheritance in the household of faith. The author of Ephesians delicately continues the parallel between establishing an earthly family and a family of faith. Roman marriage, for example, involved the husband's *manus* (lit.hand), or power or jurisdiction over the wife. In the family of God, Christ is metaphorically described at God's right hand and in possession of the ultimate *manus*, which overrides the power of every male as father, husband, master.

There is a subtle message in Ephesians: there is a new order of power. God is *Patria Potestas* (paternal family power)[28] whose authority is conveyed through Christ, the Firstborn of the family by whom Christians are now adopted as children—male and female—seated with Christ (Eph. 2:6). The position of honor accorded to Christ supersedes all earthly forms of *manus* (1:21). All peoples fall under new jurisdiction. From God as paterfamilias, every family is named and strengthened by the riches of God's glory (Eph. 3:14, 15).

The author of Ephesians has quietly rearranged the prevailing view of socio-religious order. Earthly fathers now have a Father; masters have a Master; husbands are now part of the Bride of Christ, the church.[29] In the first and second centuries, dominant groups (fathers, masters, husbands) had been the locii and determinants of the family structure in Roman and Greek society. By means of textual hints in Ephesians, Galatians, and Romans, a family of adoptees was forming in the first and second centuries to challenge even the authority of the Holy Roman Empire.

The formation of this family of adoptees is dependent upon an acceptance-of-differences by God as Adopting Father. This acceptance-of-differences is made possible by Christ Jesus. The differences portrayed in Eph. 2 are between uncircumcised/circumcised, aliens from the commonwealth of Israel / non-aliens from the commonwealth of Israel, and strangers to the covenant of promise / non-strangers to the covenant of promise. A listing of these divisions is followed by these verses of reconciliation:

> But now in Christ Jesus you who once were far off have been brought near by the blood of Christ. For he is our peace; in his flesh he has made both groups into one and has broken down the dividing wall, that is, the hostility between us. He has abolished the law with its commandments and ordinances, that he might create in himself one new humanity in place of the two, thus making peace, and might reconcile both groups to God in one body through the cross, thus putting to death that hostility through it. (Eph. 2:13–16)

In the Temple in Jerusalem, the Court of the Gentiles was separated by a balustrade or fence from the temple area for Jews. Jewish women were also set apart from Jewish men in the Women's Court and not allowed to enter the Court of Israel, reserved for Jewish men (see diagram). The statement in Eph. 2:14 that Jesus is our peace and has broken down the dividing wall ("the middle wall of partition", KJV) is often taken to refer to the barriers in the Temple of Jerusalem. The statement, "he [Jesus Christ] is our peace," thus pertains not only to Jew and Gentile, but to the barrier between men and women. Breaking down these dividing walls of partition is necessary for the formation of the adoptive family. Eph. 2:14 is also read by some not as an allusion to the actual Temple in Jerusalem, but as a reference to the divisive function of the law with its manmade statutes and ordinances. This interpretation still is valid for our purpose which is to establish a Biblical basis for the acceptance-of-differences necessary for a healthy and functional adoptive family of faith.

At Home in God's Household

Adoption is a very old topic. It can be found in the Greek myth of Zeus, who persuaded his wife Hera to adopt Heracles by taking him to her body and letting Heracles slide to earth under her robes in imitation of passage through the birth canal.[30] The cuneiform texts from the ancient Nuzi near Kirkuk in Iraq also include tablets of adoption.[31] The law codes of Babylon include Hammurabi's Code of Laws, which mentions the responsibilities of not only adopting parents, but adoptees. For example, in Code #192, we find: "If a son of a paramour or a prostitute say to his adoptive mother or father, 'You are not my father, or my mother,' his tongue shall be cut off."

The early church fathers and the later Reformers were more clement or forbearant. Irenaeus, for example, wrote that the Spirit of God did "announce that the fullness of the times of the adoption had arrived, that the kingdom of heaven and earth had drawn nigh, and that *He* was dwelling within those that believe on Him who was born Emmanuel of the Virgin."[32] Although Calvin made no allusion to adoption,[33] Luther translated the term *huiothesia* as "filial spirit" in Rom. 8:15 or as "sonship" in Romans, Galatians, and Ephesians.[34]

Not every ancient or patristic source can be cited; not every commentary has been referenced in this book. However, as we have seen by the selection of examples above, there are so many possibilities for application of the biblical doctrine of adoption that it is as if the church has been given a new concept.

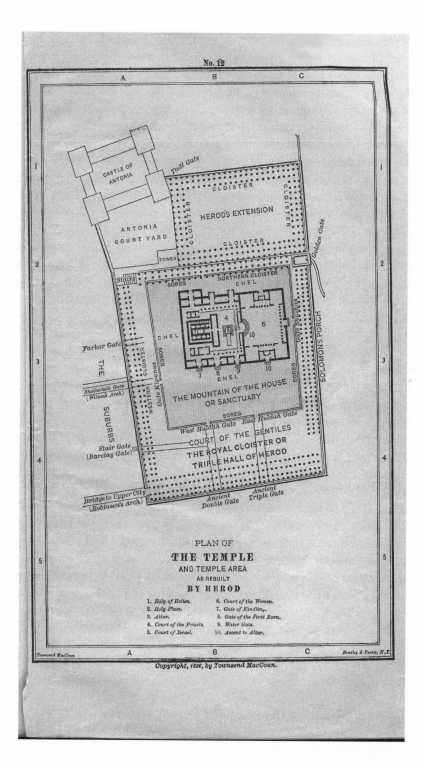

PLAN OF

THE TEMPLE

AND TEMPLE AREA

AS REBUILT

BY HEROD

1. Holy of Holies.	6. Court of the Women.
2. Holy Place.	7. Gate of Kindling.
3. Altar.	8. Gate of the First Born.
4. Court of the Priests.	9. Water Gate.
5. Court of Israel.	10. Ascent to Altar.

My goals in raising these possibilities are fourfold. First, I hope to embolden Christians to rely on a biblical, anthropological mirror to image themselves as beloved of God, as adopted sons and daughters.

Second, I want to encourage the Christian church as a family of faith to develop its ecclesiology to include a healthy acceptance-of-differences among all its members as demonstrated by resilient and flexible families in our society who have adopted children and accepted dissimilarities.

Third, I desire to support those parents who deal daily with the joys and challenges of adoption. Adoptive parents need a theology to sustain them, particularly when the way is arduous and laborious. Birth parents and adoptees need an expansive theological foundation to encompass the pain of relinquishment.

Fourth, I offer this book as a gift to adoptees in our nation of adoptees.[35] Most important of all, adoptees should know they are not second-class citizens, bastard children, unwanted, or illegitimate, but born of the womb-love of God, swaddled in God's mercy and compassion. In microcosm, they are the model, the measure of all of us in God's family.

A Larger Embrace

The actress Isabella Rossellini has expressed her experience with adoption as being a "larger embrace" of humankind, a link to the genes of all humanity, with roots in Adam and Eve. When the daughter of actress Ingrid Bergman and filmmaker Roberto Rossellini adopted a son, she was asked, "How does it feel to look at your child, knowing that none of your parents, whom the entire world adored, is in that baby?"[36] Rossellini replied quickly, "The genetic connection in adoption includes my parents and goes far beyond them, all the way back to Adam and Eve." Then, fearing she would be dismissed for this unpremeditated response, in her autobiography, she expanded on her answer: "In comparison to having a biological child—I have one of those, too—adoption carries the added dimension of connection not only to your own tribe but beyond, widening the scope of what constitutes love, ties, and family. It is a larger embrace."[37] On the adoption application, Rossellini listed no specifics, requesting simply a child, preferably non-white. Her son, part African American, brought to her, she says, a "sense of communion that breached class, cultural, and social divisions."[38] He connected her to other women, especially in the consequences of pregnancy. Rossellini became more conscious of her social privilege; she could afford to have another child.

> Adoption took me from the pedestal of my social privileges and bonded me with the realities I'd only heard about until then but had not belonged to.

Adoption connected me to other worlds and other realities. It's the "larger embrace" effect again.[39]

Largesse of heart is illustrated from a child's point of view in a comment from Quintana, a sixteen-year-old adopted child. Quintana's birth mother was eighteen when Quintana was born; her birth father was twenty-one. When she was twelve hours old, she was relinquished for adoption into the arms and hearts of her adoptive parents. She has been hesitant to look for her birth mother, although she has the support of her adoptive parents. She knows the name of her birth mother and her general location. When asked what she would do if she found her birth mother, she said, "I would put one arm around Mom and one arm around my other Mommy, and I'd say, 'Hello, Mommies.'"[40]

The "larger embrace" occurred as Milton and Julia Smith adopted seven older and special-needs children through Bethany Christian Services in Michigan. For one sibling group, they were the last stop before life in an institution. With a pervasive sense of Christian conviction, the Smiths' mutual response to the idea of taking the older and special-needs children was the query, "If we don't do it, who is going to do it?"[41] Some of the special needs included ADHD, learning disabilities, trust and attachment issues, speech and developmental delays, and drug addiction. There were many late nights for Milton and Julia Smith, tending to babies withdrawing from the influence of prenatal crack cocaine. The older children they adopted came with memories of and some attachments to their birth mothers, and Julia Smith encourages them to keep their hearts open. "I have enough love for seven children and a husband," she says. "The children can have enough love for me and their biological mother."[42] This expansion of the heart is accomplished through God's tensile grace.

Adoption: The Future of an Inclination

Sigmund Freud presented one of the most pervasive and well-developed critiques of religion in his work on the role of religion and the development of the personality, *The Future of an Illusion.* For Freud, an illusion was not so much an error as a wish that comes near to a psychiatric delusion. He believed that the psychic origin of religious ideas was infantile wish-fulfillment rooted in the terrifying impression of helplessness in childhood.[43] In other words, religion was nothing but the creation of an illusion. Freud gives an example of an infantile prototype and its "religious" continuation, writing, "For once before one has found oneself in a similar state of helplessness: as a small child, in relation to one's parents. One had reason to fear them, and especially one's father."[44]

The "material of memories of the helplessness" of early childhood, he argued, creates a store of ideas, religious in the widest sense.[45] The frightened child, who later became the anxious adult, clung to a benevolent, protecting, and divine Providence more powerful than the earthly father and other causes of neurosis. At the nucleus of every divine figure, including the idea of a single God, stood the father. "Now that God was a single person, man's relations to him could recover the intimacy and intensity of the child's relation to his father. But if one had done so much for one's father, one wanted to have a reward, or at least to be his only beloved child, his Chosen People."[46]

Freud mourned for his birthplace, Freiberg in Moravia. In 1931, when he was seventy-five, the mayor of Freiberg unveiled a bronze tablet at his birthplace. In a letter of thanks, Freud commented, "Deep within me, covered over, there still lives that happy child from Freiberg, the first-born son of a youthful mother, who had received the first indelible impressions from this air, from this soil."[47] Such indelible impressions form on the soul as spirit (*die Seele*), not on the soul as a psychological concept, as Freud himself used the term *die Geist*, the psyche or that which is most valuable to a person while alive.[48] Spiritually, the desire to return "home" becomes the future of an inclination, and in that sense, it is wish fulfillment. It is based on a preconscious awareness and inclination to return to the nurturing Creator. The fetus in utero has a sense of the movement, rhythm, smell, and relatedness to the one who carries. It is primal wish-fulfillment to be surrounded by safe, fluid, nourishing uterine waters.

It is the desire of many mystics, saints, and ordinary Christians to be embraced once again by the One who ultimately carries them in love, in womb-love, the compassion and mercy of God. The basis of Christian faith becomes not the terrifying impression of helplessness in childhood[49] as Freud alleged, but rather the awesome imprint of primal connectedness. This preconscious awareness is the beginning of the future of an inclination, a search and reunion with the Creator. This is not the infantile thinking Freud would decry. It is the search of all Christians as adoptees for knowledge of the One to whom they are precious.

> O LORD, you have searched me and known me.
> For it was you who formed my inward parts;
> you knit me together in my mother's womb.
>
> (Ps. 139:1, 13)

Notes

EPIGRAPH

1. 1 Sam. 1:20
2. 1 Sam. 1:27
3. Luke 23:29
4. John 19:26–27
5. 1 John 3:1

INTRODUCTION

1. Biblical scholars Kathryn L. Roberts and John E. Alsup suggest the usage of other words besides "family" for the community of faith described in such texts as Ephesians. For some, who have had abusive experiences with families, there will be a negative association. John Alsup recommends *oikos*, which can be translated "household" and is consistent with my reliance on the book of Ephesians. See John Alsup, "Die Kirche als OIKOS entdecken," *Kirche und Volk Gottes: Festschrift fuer Juergen Roloff zum 70.Geburtstag* (Neukirchener Verlag, 2001), 110–31.

2. Biblical scholar Phyllis Trible has developed this maternal metaphor of God by connecting two Hebrew words with the same root [*rhm*]: "womb" (*rehem*) and the adjective "merciful" or compassionate (*rahum*). The latter word, (rahum), is used exclusively for the Creator God, never for creatures. Trible uses the term "womb-love" as a translation of the Hebrew term *rahum*, which means God's love and compassion. See Phyllis Trible, *God and the Rhetoric of Sexuality* (Philadelphia: Fortress Press, 1978), 51.

3. Don Browning et al., eds. in *From Culture Wars to Common Ground,* 2d ed. (Louisville, Ky.: Westminster John Knox Press, 2000), 315. The church is called upon to develop "a bilingual theology and a bifocal program that supports intact families and addresses the realities of other family forms."

4. David M. Brodzinsky and Marshall D. Schechter, eds., *The Psychology of Adoption* (Oxford: Oxford University Press, 1990).

5. See H. David Kirk, *Shared Fate: A Theory of Adoption and Mental Health* (New York: The Free Press of Glencoe, 1964) and Adam Pertman, *Adoption Nation: How the Adoption Revolution Is Transforming America* (New York: Basic Books, 2000).

6. Joyce Maguire Pavao, *The Family of Adoption* (Boston: Beacon Press, 1998), xiii.

7. Browning, *From Culture Wars,* 301. The transformative view does not repress family affections.

8. Douglas Tzan raised an important issue in regard to my use of the term "gift of a child." In response to my article titled "Womb-love: The Practice and Theology of Adoption" in *Christian Century* (January 24, 2001): 10–13, Tzan writes: "Calling a child a 'gift from God' not only perpetuates the unhealthy myth of the 'chosen baby' but also gives it a holy patina: the adoptee is still not born, but is brought by God instead of the stork." "Being Adopted" (letters), *Christian Century* (March 21–28, 2001): 45–46.

I do not want my use of the term "gift" to be misinterpreted as objectifying a child or as denying a child as much information as possible about their birth and delivery, birth parents, and birth family history. I am using the term "gift" to distinguish it from "creation"; adoptive parents are aware they have not produced or created a child. Most importantly, I am using the term "gift" to capture the sense of being deeply wanted and loved. In therapeutic circles, we feel it essential that a child see a gleam in someone's eye, focus on a doting face, absorb the beam of pride in the eyes of a significant beholder. A child needs this sense of being "beloved." Optimally, this sense is conveyed by a primary caretaker(s). When the caretakers are adoptive parents, their perception of the "beloved" (the adopted child) is as precious gift. This sense is not intended to lay a burden on the adoptee. It is a type of blessing, an utterance of thanks.

9. Kirk, *Shared Fate,* 59.

10. Ibid.

11. See Robert Alexander Webb, *The Reformed Doctrine of Adoption* (Grand Rapids: Wm. B. Eerdmans, 1947).

12. Vivian B. Shapiro, Janet R. Shapiro, and Isabel H. Paret, *Complex Adoption & Assisted Reproductive Technology* (New York: The Guilford Press, 2001), 16.

CHAPTER 1: THE TREMBLING WOMB

1. This is Phyllis Trible's translation of Jer. 31:20. See *God and the Rhetoric of Sexuality* (Philadelphia: Fortress Press, 1978), 45. The root word is [*rhm*] for both womb-love [*rechem*] and God's compassion or mercy [*rahum*].

2. Fred Craddock, in a taped conversation to Jeanne Stevenson-Moessner.

3. David M. Brodzinsky, "Adjustment to Adoption: A Psychosocial Perspective," *Clinical Psychology Review* 7 (1987): 25-47, and David M. Brodzinsky, "A Stress and Coping Model of Adoption Adjustment," in *The Psychology of Adoption*, ed. Brodzinsky and Schechter (Oxford: Oxford University Press, 1990), 3.

4. E. James Anthony, M.D., in the Foreword to *The Psychology of Adoption*, ibid.

5. Ann M. Martin, *Karen's School Picture* (New York: Scholastic, 1989), 60–62.

6. Nelle Morton, *The Journey Is Home* (Boston: Beacon Press, 1985), 31.

7. Christine Swientek, *Was Adoptivkinder wissen sollten und wie man es ihnen sagen kann* (*What Adopted Children Should Know and How They Can Be Told*) (Freiburg: Herder, 1993), 116–17 (my translation).

8. Gerald Bonner, *God's Decree and Man's Destiny: Studies on the Thought of Augustine of Hippo* (London: Variorum Reprints, 1987), 495–514.

9. Ibid., 512. See also Augustine, *Expositions of the Psalms 33-50* (*Enarrationes in Psalmos*), trans. Maria Boulding, *The Works of Saint Augustine* series (Hyde Park: New City Press, 2000), 381, for Ps.49:2. See Augustine, *Sermons III/5 (148–183) on the New Testament*, trans. Edmund Hill, *The Works of Saint Augustine* series, (New Rochelle: New City Press, 1992), 209 (Serm. 166, 4–7).

10. *Westminster Confession of Faith* (1647), 6.074, Chapter XIV/Chapter XII. See *Book of Confessions* (New York: The General Assembly of the Presbyterian Church (U.S.A.), 1983).

11. Sigmund Freud, "From the History of an Infantile Neurosis" (1918) in *Collected Papers, Vol. III*, Case Histories (New York: Basic Books, 1959), 597.

12. Norel C. Waldhaus, "Our Gift," in *Perspectives on a Grafted Tree*, ed. Patricia Irwin Johnston (Fort Wayne, Ind.: Perspectives Press, 1983), 65.

13. Nancy Newton Verrier, *The Primal Wound: Understanding the Adopted Child* (Baltimore: Gateway Press, 1994).

14. Norel C.Waldhaus, "Our Gift," in *Perspectives on a Grafted Tree*, ed. Patricia Irwin Johnston (Fort Wayne, Ind.: Perspectives Press, 1983), 65.

15. Phyllis Trible, *God and the Rhetoric of Sexuality*, 51. See also J. A. Clanton, *In Whose Image? God and Gender* (New York: Crossroad, 1990), 23.

16. Trible, *God and the Rhetoric of Sexuality*, 53. This is Trible's translation, which is comparable to Jer. 31:20c.

CHAPTER 2: GIVE ME CHILDREN, OR I SHALL DIE!

1. Joan Liebman-Smith, *In Pursuit of Pregnancy: How Couples Discover, Cope with, and Resolve Their Fertility Problems* (New York: Newmarket Press, 1987).

2. Jon D. Levenson, "The Tree of Life: The Loss, Recovery, and Redefinition of Immortality in Judaism and Christianity," Henry Luce III Fellow presentation, Princeton, N. J., November 3, 2000.

3. Michael Gold, "Adoption: A New Problem for Jewish Law," *Judaism* 36 (fall 1987): 446.

4. For example, if Gold were a *levi* or *kohen* (a special category of priests), his son would still be a *yisrael*, a lower class. Gold's daughter is restricted as a convert from marrying into a higher class.

5. Gold, 445.

6. Others such as Francis Lyall do not consider Naomi's *in loco parentis* of Obed as an adoptive relationship (see Lyall, "Roman Law in the Writings of Paul—Adoption," *The Journal of Biblical Literature* 88, [1969]: 463.)

7. Francis Lyall, 463.

8. Lyall, 267: "During the period of the Roman Republic, Romans did not generally believe that a living person could be a god. However, during the last century B.C.E. the Republic's expanding empire came into contact with many peoples, such as the Egyptians, who did hold such beliefs. The growing acceptance of such beliefs within Roman society was evidenced by the fact that when Julius Caesar was assassinated in 44 B.C.E., many Romans were willing to believe that he had undergone an apotheosis at death, being raised up as god." Although Augustus did not encourage divine honors during his lifetime, he did not discourage belief about divinization after death.

9. This title was used by all later Roman emperors. See Ralph Martin Novak, *Christianity and the Roman Empire: Background Texts* (Harrisburg, Penn.: Trinity Press, 2001), 10.

CHAPTER 3: CONCEPTION IN THE BARREN PLACES

1. Maxine Rosenberg, *Being Adopted* (New York: Lothrop, Lee & Shepard Books, 1984), epilogue. Transracial adoption has engendered controversy. For example, in 1972, the National Association of Black Social Workers adopted the position that black children should only be placed in black families. See Dawn Day's *The Adoption of Black Children: Counteracting Institutional Discrimination* (Lexington, Mass.: Lexington Books, 1979), 98. In 1973, in response to this position, the Child Welfare League of America changed its standards to read that it is preferable to place children in families of their own racial background. As domestic

transracial adoption has engendered strong reactions such as these, international adoptions are on the increase.

2. Bruce M. Rappaport, *The Open Adoption Book: A Guide to Adoption Without Tears* (New York: Macmillan, 1992), 56.

3. Mary Calloway, *Sing, O Barren One: A Study in Comparative Midrash* SBL Dissertation Series 91 (Atlanta: Scholars Press, 1986), 135.

4. Ibid., 4.

5. Ibid., 33.

6. Ibid., 59.

7. Ibid., 112.

8. H. David Kirk, *Shared Fate: A Theory of Adoption and Mental Health* (New York: The Free Press of Glencoe, 1964), 33.

CHAPTER 4: EXPECTANT WAITING

1. Adam Pertman, *Adoption Nation: How the Adoption Revolution Is Transforming America* (New York: Basic Books, 2000), 43.

2. Ibid., 43.

3. Ibid., 10.

CHAPTER 5: HOMECOMING

1. William Fisch, "The Way I Found My Father," *Julien's Journal* 27, no. 6 (2002): 20.

2. Ibid., 21.

3. Ed Loring, "The Prodigal Daughter," in *Hospitality* 20, no. 2 (2001): 3.

4. Henri J. M. Nouwen, *The Return of the Prodigal Son: A Story of Homecoming* (New York: Doubleday, 1992), 6.

5. Vivian B. Shapiro, Janet R. Shapiro, Isabel H. Paret, "International Adoption and Family Formation," in *Complex Adoption and Assisted Reproductive Technology: A Developmental Approach to Clinical Practice* (New York: The Guilford Press, 2001), 108.

CHAPTER 6: GROWING PAINS

1. Joyce Maguire Pavao, *The Family of Adoption* (Boston: Beacon Press, 1998), 60.

2. Elaine Frank and Gloria Hochan, "Adoption and the Stages of Development," National Adoption Information Clearinghouse, 1990. The article can be obtained on the Internet: http:www.calib.com/naic/pubs/f_stages.htm.

3. H. David Kirk, *Shared Fate: A Theory of Adoption and Mental Health* (New York: The Free Press of Glencoe, 1964), 160.

4. Betty Jane Lifton, *Twice Born: Memoirs of an Adopted Daughter* (New York: St. Martin's Griffin, 1977), 252. It was actually Robert J. Lifton, psychiatrist, who created the term *twice born* for adoptees: "I would say that if one is twice born, one has to carve out a new self distinct from the one society assigned you."

5. Erik Erikson, *Identity: Youth and Crisis* (New York: W. W. Norton & Co.,1968).

6. Jeanne Stevenson Moessner, "Cultural Dissolution: 'I Lost Africa'," *Missiology: An International Review* XIV, 3 (1986).

7. Carol Gilligan, *In a Different Voice: Psychological Theory and Women's Development* (Cambridge, Mass.:Harvard University Press,1982).

8. Valentina P. Wasson, *The Chosen Baby* (New York: J. B. Lippincott, 1939).

9. Paul M. Brinich, "Adoption from the Inside Out: A Psychoanalytic Perspective," in *The Psychology of Adoption* (New York: Oxford University Press, 1990), 61.

10. Ibid., 45.

11. Ibid., 52.

12. Ibid., 45.

13. Kirk, *Shared Fate*, 162–63.

14. John Boswell, *The Kindness of Strangers* (New York: Vintage Books, 1988), 21.

15. Ibid., 24.

16. Ibid., 165.

17. Ronald J. Nydam, "Adoption and the Image of God," *Journal of Pastoral Care* 46, no.3 (1992): 256.

18. Ronald J. Nydam, "Character Disorders: Where Faith and Healing Sometimes Fail," *Journal of Pastoral Care* 45, no.2 (1991): 142. For a more thorough treatment of birth parent loss and identity formation, see Nydam, *Adoptees Come of Age: Living within Two Families* (Louisville, Ky.: Westminster / John Knox Press, 1999).

19. Angela Herrell, "His Great Plan," *LifeLines* 6, no.4 (2001):10,11.

20. Florence Clothier, "The Psychology of the Adopted Child," *Mental Hygiene* 27 (1943): 229.

21. Lifton, *Twice Born*, 98.

22. Ibid., 33.

23. Ibid., 219.

24. Ibid., 250.

25. Ibid.

26. Betty Jane Lifton, *Lost and Found: The Adoption Experience* (New York: The Dial Press, 1983), 273.

27. David M. Brodzinsky, "A Stress and Coping Model of Adoption Adjustment, in *The Psychology of Adoption,* ed. Brodzinsky and Schechter (Oxford: Oxford University Press, 1990), 16.

28. Ibid., 3.

29. Ibid.

30. Nydam, "Adoption and the Image of God," 256.

31. The absence of the feminine dimension to the "family of faith" is striking. I have developed elsewhere the thesis that the mother of God in the person of Mary was not mentioned by the author due to the reaction in the Mediterranean to the cult of the Great Mother, manifested in Ephesus as Great Artemis. Whatever the reason for this omission, the divine family constituted through adoption is paralleled to the Divine Family of the Holy Roman Empire, ruled over by a Divine Father or emperor of the Julio-Claudian dynasty. All were adopted after Caesar Augustus, as mentioned earlier. Thus, the adoptive family constituted in Ephesians is contrasted to the royal family in the Holy Roman Empire.

32. Bruce J. Malina, *The Social Gospel of Jesus: The Kingdom of God in Mediterranean Perspective* (Minneapolis: Fortress Press, 2001), 153. See also Philip F. Esler, " 'Keeping It in the Family': Culture, Kinship and Identity in I Thessalonians and Galatians," in *Families & Family Relations as Represented in Early Judaisms and Early Christianities: Texts and Fictions* (Leiden: Deo Publishing, 2000), 145–84. In the ancient Mediterranean world, the basic social distinction was between kin and non-kin. In Galatians, fictive kinship is created through God the Father's adoption of children through baptism. These children, whether Gentile converts or Israelite Christ-followers, are children of the promise made to Sarah in Galatians 4:21–31.

33. Malina, *The Social Gospel of Jesus,* 159.

34. Henri J. M. Nouwen, *The Return of the Prodigal Son: A Story of Homecoming* (New York: Doubleday, 1992), 97.

35. Daniel L. Schutte, "Here I Am, Lord," in *The Presbyterian Hymnal* (Louisville, Ky.: Westminster/John Knox Press, 1990), 525.

CHAPTER 7: A THEOLOGY OF ADOPTION

1. Anna Case-Winters, *God's Power: Traditional Understandings & Contemporary Challenges* (Louisville, Ky,: Westminster/John Knox Press, 1990), 192.

2. Carter Heyward in *Our Passion for Justice: Images of Power, Sexuality, and Liberation* (New York: Pilgrim Press, 1984); Jill Raitt et al., ed. in *Christian Spirituality: High Middle Ages and Reformation* (New York: Crossroads, 1987); Sallie McFague in *Models of God: Theology for an Ecological, Nuclear Age* (Minneapolis: Fortress Press, 1989); and Elizabeth A. Johnson in *She Who Is: The Mystery of God in Feminist Theological Discourse* (New York: Crossroads, 1993) have written as feminist theologians on power as relational bonding.

3. Phyllis Trible, *God and the Rhetoric of Sexuality* (Philadelphia: Fortress Press, 1978), 51.

4. Sue Walker, "To Mama," in *Perspectives on a Grafted Tree: Thoughts for Those Touched by Adoption*, ed. Patricia Irwin Johnston (Fort Wayne, Ind.: Perspectives Press, 1983), 118.

5. Martin E. Marty, *A Cry of Absence: Reflections for the Winter of the Heart* (San Francisco: Harper & Row, 1983), 134–35.

6. I am indebted to Rev. Stephen Kolmetz for his insights on his faith journey as an adoptee, insights which I have incorporated into my comments. Stephen Kolmetz, "The Cabbage Patch Gospel: Adoption and Spiritual/Theological Formation," May 11, 1995.

7. Ibid., 6.

8. Ibid., 7.

9. Ibid., 8.

10. Ibid., 9.

11. Ibid., 10–11.

12. In his article "On Divine Perfection," examining classical and neoclassical views of God, William L. Power develops the divine attribute of the pathos of God. Citing recent philosophers and theologians—Charles Hartshorne, Oscar Cullmann, Nicholas Wolterstorff, Richard Swinburne, and Schubert Ogden—who have argued "that the classical understanding of God's eternity is inadequate and have sought to replace it with a notion of eternity as infinite temporality" (*Anglican Theological Review* LXXV:1, 37), William Power presents mutability as a fundamental attribute of God. God is omnipassable, i.e. "God is epistemically affected or influenced by the whole of creation" (44). God's impassibility is given up; instead, God is understood as receptive to the world's influence. "Since the early nineteenth century, numerous theologians and biblical scholars, and philosophers of religion have criticized the doctrine of divine impassibility." (Warren McWilliams in *The Passion of God: Divine Suffering in Contemporary Protestant Theology* [Macon, Ga.: Mercer Univ. Press, 1985]; McWilliams illustrates the contemporary interpretations of God's passion in this work of theologians Juergen Moltmann, James Cone, Geddes MacGregor, Kazoh Kitamori, Daniel Day Williams, Jung Young Lee. Various aspects of the debate are illustrated in McWilliams's chapter 1, which includes patristic theologians.)

13. Cynthia Rigby, *Catalyst* 27, no.2 (2001): 8.

14. Henri J. M. Nouwen in *The Wounded Healer: Ministry in Contemporary Society* (Garden City, N.Y.: Doubleday, 1979), 81–82.

15. Nicholas Wolterstorff, *Lament for a Son* (Grand Rapids: Wm. B. Eerdmans, 1987), 81.

16. Bo Reicke, *Re-examining Paul's Letters: The History of the Pauline Correspondence*, ed. David P. Moessner and Ingalisa Reicke (Harrisburg, Pa.: Trinity Press, 2001).

17. David Kirk, *Adoptive Kinship: A Modern Institution in Need of Reform* (Toronto: Butterworths, 1981), 65.

CHAPTER 8: A BIBLICAL EMBRACE

1. Katheryn Pfisterer Darr, *Far More Precious than Jewels: Perspectives on Biblical Women* (Louisville, Ky.: Westminster/John Knox Press, 1991), 188.

2. The verb for *adopted* or *took* in its root form is *lkch,* a common verb in Hebrew with ten distinct meanings. The Septuagint uses the word *paideuo,* which can connote a sense of upbringing, discipline, and education. It is the same word used in Eph. 6:4, addressed to fathers: "Fathers, do not provoke your children to anger, but *bring them up* in the discipline and instruction of the Lord."

3. Jon D. Levenson, *Esther: A Commentary* (Louisville, Ky.: Westminster John Knox Press, 1997), 58. Although the precise nature of Mordecai's adoption of Esther is not known, Levenson objects to the Greek version and rabbinic midrashim that sees the relationship as one of marriage. Levenson views this reading as a desire to avoid the thought that a Jew married a Gentile. Levenson regards Mordecai as a "foster father."

4. James M. Scott, *Adoption as Sons of God: An Exegetical Investigation into the Background of Huiothesia in the Pauline Corpus* (Tuebingen: J. C. B. Mohr, 1992), 268.

5. Sidnie White Crawford, "Esther," in *Women in Scripture: A Dictionary of Named and Unnamed Women in the Hebrew Bible, the Apocryphal/Deuterocanonical Books, and the New Testament* (Boston: Houghton Mifflin 2000), 75.

6. K. Pfisterer Darr, *Far More Precious,* 170.

7. Jon D. Levenson, "The Tree of Life: The Loss, Recovery, and Redefinition of Immortality in Judaism and Christianity," Henry Luce Fellow presentation, Princeton, N.J., November 3, 2000.

8. Sigmund Freud, "On the Universal Tendency to Debasement in the Sphere of Love," in Vol. II of the *Standard Edition of the Complete Psychological Works of Sigmund Freud,* trans. James Strachey and Anna Freud (London: Hogarth Press, 1953–1974), 189.

9. Peter Gay, *Freud: A Life for Our Time* (New York: W. W. Norton, 1988), 515.

10. Joachim Scharfenberg, *Sigmund Freud & His Critique of Religion* (Philadelphia: Fortress Press, 1968), 24.

11. Ibid., 145.

12. Harold Kelman, introduction to *Feminine Psychology,* by Karen Horney (New York: W. W. Norton 1967), 9.

13. Gay, *Freud: A Life for Our Time,* 5.

14. Ibid., 6.

15. Ibid., 7.

16. The term *huiothesia* in the secular usage of Hellenistic Greek means "adoption" or adoption as sons and daughters. There is a growing body of research on the origin of this term, its usage and implications. See James M. Scott, *Adoption as Sons of God*; see also Brendan Byrne, *"Sons of God"—Seed of Abraham* (Rome: Biblical Institute Press, 1979).

17. Charles B. Cousar, *Galatians,* Interpretation (Atlanta: John Knox Press, 1971), 105. Cousar regards the comparison of Hagar and Sarah as not only an allegorical interpretation of the Hagar-Sarah story, but as midrash or an exposition of Scripture—a commentary on the *torah.* "He [Paul] provides a *midrash* on the Genesis text in the sense that his commentary has to do with the situation of the Gentiles in the Galatian context. He shows that the ancient story of Hagar and Sarah still has a function. It sheds light on the issue of circumcision facing Gentile converts."

18. The danger is the legitimization of slavery; Hagar, the slave of Sarah, is taken as the foremother of African Americans. The same world-view that maintained descendants of Ham were meant to be slaves could erroneously be operative here.

19. See Hans Dieter Betz, *Galatians: A Commentary on Paul's Letter to the Churches in Galatia* (Philadelphia: Fortress Press, 1979), 239. Betz views the pericope containing the Hagar and Sarah material as allegory and typology, citing James Barr, *Old and New in Interpretation* (London: SCM, 1966), 110ff. By typology, he means taking historical material as prototypical of present events, institutions, and persons.

Betz also quotes Nietzsche as calling this allegory of Hagar and Sarah "this unheard-of philological farce in regard to the Old Testament." See Friedrich Nietzsche, *Morgenroete*, in *Werke* (Darmstadt: Wissenschaftliche Buchgesellschaft, 1963) 1.1068, quoted by Hans Joachim Schoeps, *Paul: The Theology of the Apostle in the Light of Jewish Religious History*, trans. Harold Knight (Philadelphia: Westminster, 1961); (Tuebingen: Mohr, Siebeck, 1959), 235.

Betz includes the correspondence of concepts given by H. Lietzmann in the *Theological Dictionary of the New Testament* 7.669 (Lietzmann, Burton, Oepke, Delling), which comes the closest to my own depiction of the lineage and legacy of Hagar and Sarah. For Leitzman, Hagar is linked through Ishmael (her son "according to the flesh") to the old covenant, Sinai, the present Jerusalem, slavery, and Judaism "according to the flesh." Sarah is linked through Isaac (her son "through the promise") to the new covenant, the heavenly Jerusalem, freedom, and Christianity "according to the Spirit."

20. Pheme Perkins, *Abraham's Divided Children: Galatians and the Politics of Faith* (Harrisburg, Pa.: Trinity Press, 2001), 84.

21. J. Louis Martyn, "The Apocalyptic Gospel in Galatians," *Interpretation* (July 2000): 255.

22. Richard Hays, *Echoes of Scripture in the Letters of Paul* (New Haven, Conn.: Yale University Press, 1989), 120.

23. Jan L. Waldron, *Giving Away Simone: A Memoir* (New York: Random House, 1995), xvi, xvii. Waldron spoke out of her pain of relinquishing her daughter: "I am tired of the willful romanticizing and reactionary rhetoric the experience seems to spawn. The legal appropriation of a child is hardly an isolated act, free from history and emotional aftermath. The word we use, *adoption*, describes merely one part of a complicated experience. Our collective rejection of the other parts and people—which include birthrelations, surrender, and often search and reunion—[eliminates] significant phases of the same experience. In this country we are having a terrible time confronting the whole story, in all its sorrow, joy, and turmoil."

24. E. Elizabeth Johnson, "Romans 9–11: The Faithfulness and Impartiality of God," in *Romans,* Pauline Theology, vol. III (Minneapolis: Fortress Press, 1995), 219.

25. Stephen Benko, *Pagan Rome and the Early Christians* (Bloomington, Ind.: Indiana University Press, 1984), 21.

26. George B. Caird, *Paul's Letters from Prison* (Oxford: Oxford University Press, 1976), 88.

27. Mary Rose D'Angelo, "Early Christian Sexual Politics and Roman Imperial Family Values: Rereading Christ and Culture," in *Papers of the Henry Luce III Fellows in Theology*, ed. Christopher I. Wilkins, vol. 6 (Philadelphia: Association of Theological Schools, forthcoming), 1–26.

28. Percy Ellwood Corbett, *The Roman Law of Marriage* (London: Oxford University Press, 1930).

29. Catherine Gonzalez and Justo Gonzalez, *Liberation Preaching: The Pulpit and the Oppressed* (Nashville: Abingdon, 1980), 88. Note: I have added "father" to their list.

30. Diodorus Siculus, 4:39:2, as cited by W. V. Martitz in Gerhard Friedrich and Gerhard Kittel, eds., *Theological Dictionary of the New Testament*, vol. 8, trans. and ed. Geoffrey W. Bromiley (Grand Rapids: Wm. B. Eerdmans, 1977), 398.

31. J. van Seters, "The Problem of Childlessness in Near Eastern Law and the Patriarchs of Israel," *Journal of Biblical Literature* 87 (1968): 404.

32. Irenaeus, *Irenaeus Against Heresies,* 3.21.4 in Alexander Roberts and James J. Donaldson, eds., *Ante-Nicene Fathers*, vol. 1 (New York: The Christian Literature Co., 1896), 452.

33. Robert A. Webb, *The Reformed Doctrine of Adoption* (Grand Rapids: Wm. B. Eerdmans, 1947), 17.

34. See J. Theodore Mueller, "Adoption," *Christianity Today* (April 27, 1962): 735. Mueller translates "filial spirit" from Luther's *kindlicher Geist* and "sonship" from *Kindschaft.*
Note: The discussion of adoption by the church fathers and in this book is not to be confused with the heresy of adoptionism held by the Ebionites. This heresy maintained that Jesus was rewarded by God for his perfect obedience and was promoted or adopted to be Son of God.

35. Adam Pertman, *Adoption Nation: How the Adoption Revolution Is Transforming America* (New York: Basic Books, 2000).

36. Isabella Rossellini, *Some of Me* (New York: Random House, 1997), 151.

37. Ibid., 152.

38. Ibid., 154.

39. Ibid., 154.

40. Jill Kremetz, *How It Feels to Be Adopted* (New York: Alfred Knopf, 1988), 61.

41. Suzanne Parks, "Angels in Adoption," in *Life Lines* 6, no. 3 (Grand Rapids: Bethany Christian Services, 2001), 5.

42. Ibid., 6.

43. Sigmund Freud, *The Future of an Illusion* (Garden City, N.Y.: Doubleday, 1961), 47.

44. Ibid., 23.

45. Ibid., 25–26.

46. Ibid., 23.

47. Peter Gay, *Freud,* 9.

48. Bruno Bettelheim, *Freud and Man's Soul* (New York: Vintage Books, 1982), 76–77. When Freud uses the word *soul*, he is not speaking about a religious phenomenon, but a psychological concept, a metaphor. For Freud, the soul was the seat of the mind and the passions. Bettelheim maintains that whereas the American usage of the word *soul* has been restricted to the sphere of religion, the correct translation for *soul* as that which is spiritual in man/woman is *die Seele.* This is not a concept or word that Freud would have used as an atheist.

49. Peter Gay, *Freud,* 9.

Index of Scriptural References

Index of Names

Index of Subjects